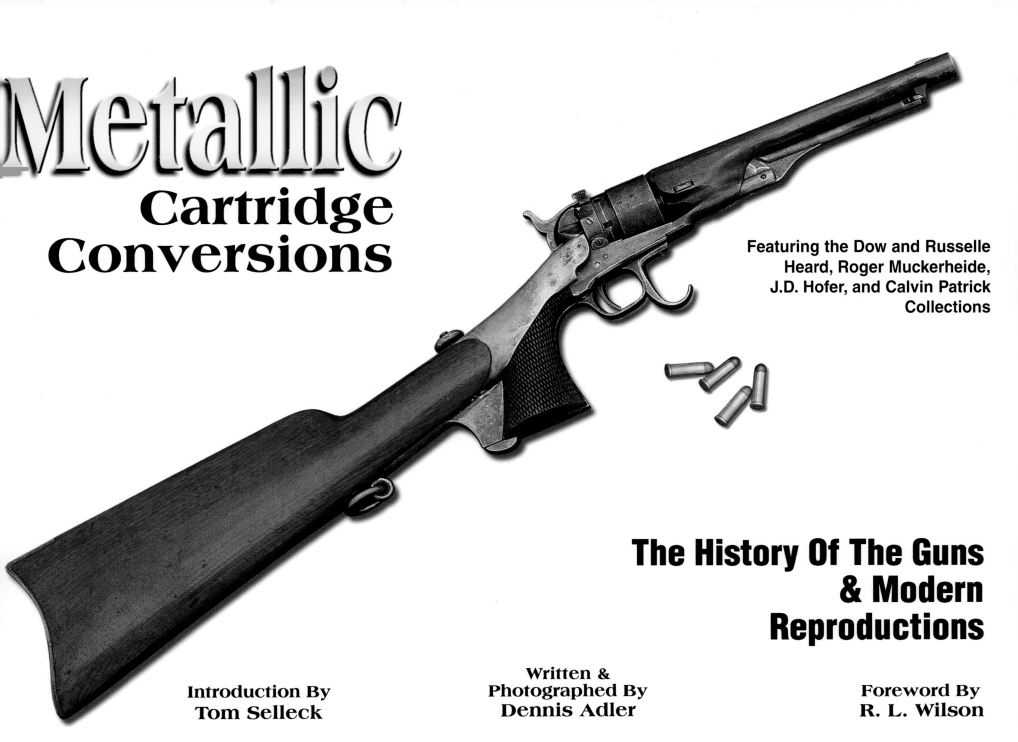

Metallic
Cartridge
Conversions

**Featuring the Dow and Russelle
Heard, Roger Muckerheide,
J.D. Hofer, and Calvin Patrick
Collections**

The History Of The Guns
& Modern
Reproductions

**Introduction By
Tom Selleck**

**Written &
Photographed By
Dennis Adler**

**Foreword By
R. L. Wilson**

Published by

 **krause publications**
An F&W Publications Company

700 East State Street • Iola, WI 54990-0001
715-445-2214 • 888-457-2873
www.krause.com

Please call or write for our free catalog of publications. Our
toll-free number to place an order or obtain a free catalog is
(800) 258-0929.

Library of Congress Catalog Number: 2002107608
ISBN: 0-87349-337-0

Printed in China

Dedication

To Jeanne, who has been the inspiration for every book I have ever written, the very heart of me for the best years of my life and my biggest fan, and to my friend Larry Wilson, without whose help I would not have a second writing career in the firearms field.

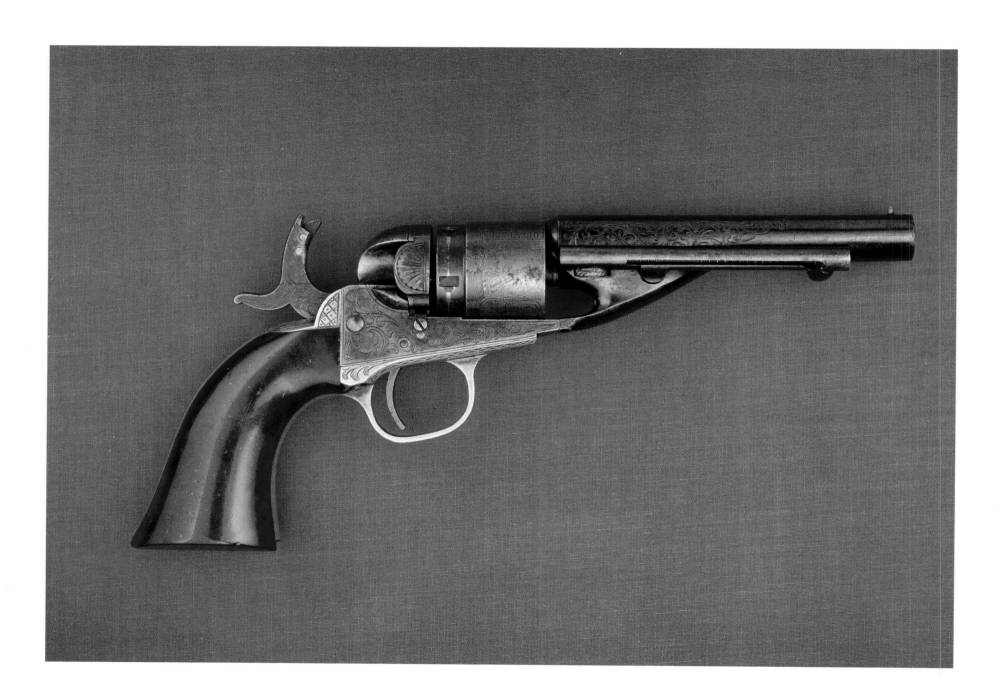

Table of Contents

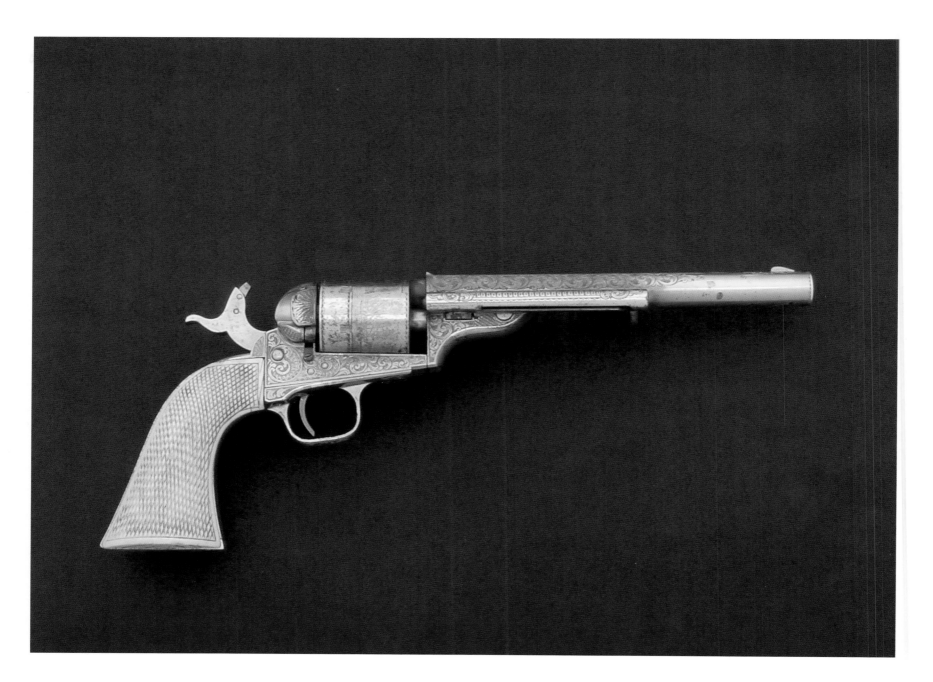

Foreword

Through his previous works on firearms — as with his numerous titles on collector cars — Dennis Adler is creating a library of books of his own authorship. With their trademark combination of lively and informative text, accompanied by rich and beautiful photographs, these titles are a must for any enthusiast of these captivating subjects.

In *Metallic Cartridge Conversions* he has created a book for any devotee of fine firearms, made by Colt's and others, and Americana. Here is a theme that has never been given its due. A great many collectors of Colt's and its competitors are percussion specialists — while an even greater number concentrate on cartridge arms. In the conversions, there is overlap with both. Since not a few were altered by non-factory gunsmiths, the field challenges the eye and the expertise of the collector, dealer, student and curator.

That means there can be pitfalls for all. *Metallic Cartridge Conversions* celebrates these ingenious creations — veritable pioneers to the post-Samuel Colt era — through exquisite illustrations, and thorough, analytical, and expository text. The models and variations are documented through specimens from some of the greatest of private and public collections. In the process of photography, Dennis Adler has had the added advantage of the expertise and experience of each collector, as credited in the pages that follow.

Because all of the models of conversions (at least by Colt's) are based on guns originally produced in Samuel Colt's lifetime, there is a direct connection of these arms with that historic inventor, entrepreneur, showman and marketing genius. Thinking in terms of the automobile, one can easily compare these conversions to the late models of Ferraris, converting into the high-tech computer age, just entering into production as founder Enzo Ferrari died.

Colt and Ferrari had a lot in common. It may easily be said that Colt is the Ferrari of the firearms line. There are more than a few owners of Ferraris who are keen on Colts, and *vice versa*. Both founders and both brands symbolize technology, craftsmanship, artistry, adventure, daring, romance and excitement.

It is particularly fitting, therefore, that the author of *Metallic Cartridge Conversions* is very much at home in the worlds of cars and of guns. In company with our good friends Steve Fjestad (of Blue Book Publications) and Luigi Chinetti, Jr. (of the North American Racing Team, importers and racers of Ferraris est. 1949), we made a pilgrimage to Ferrari in 1998. Besides having the full factory tour, Dennis tested new cars, including the F 355 F1, and was able to photograph and drive on Fiorano, the official test and racing track in Maranello.

Dennis Adler is representative of the close association between the worlds of automobiles and firearms. It is a great pleasure to see that he continues to produce his unique brand of publications on cars, joined by his growing series of equally stylish and informative books on guns.

In *Metallic Cartridge Conversions*, he has created yet another first-rate work, not only for the Colt aficionado and the lover of other makes of guns and of Americana, but, as is also true in his car books, for anyone who is keen on a related and greatly treasured collectible: fine books.

Congratulations are in order for *Metallic Cartridge Conversions*. Along with thousands of other devotees, I look forward to many more of Dennis Adler's tomes on guns — and on cars — which are sure to come in the future.

R.L. Wilson

Introduction

Inspecting the ivory-stocked, Colt cartridge conversion pistol, Paul Cable takes in the intricate engraving, reads his name inscribed on the backstrap and says to his wife, "Your father's a real artist." Cable is a character from the movie *Last Stand at Saber River*, and the gun he is admiring is a Colt 1860 Army .44 caliber Richards-type cartridge conversion, a model commonly seen in the post Civil War era and throughout the 1870s.

Cartridge conversion firearms played an important role in the post-Civil War era, but in that simple statement Cable connects past and present. One reason cartridge conversion firearms were important in the past and why they are still valued today is that they are indeed works of art. In his book *Metallic Cartridge Conversions*, author and photographer Dennis Adler ties the past and the present together by detailing the rich history surrounding the evolution of conversion firearms and writing about the increasing public awareness and interest in collecting original models and modern-day reproductions. Through the text and photography in this book, readers cannot help but have impressed upon them a sense of appreciation for the depth of history attached to these firearms, and the craftsmanship required to create these remarkable, handcrafted revolvers.

The post-Civil War era and settling of the American West represent a transitional period in our nation's history, and the conversion revolver was a key piece of that eventful time. Soldiers came home from the war changed. America was expanding farther and farther west and manufacturing technology had made great strides during the 1860s to accommodate the war's demand for better firearms. This technology allowed mass production of percussion firearms throughout the war years creating a surplus of percussion pistols in the late 1860s that would later be converted to fire the new self-contained metallic cartridge.

Percussion firearms were converted largely because there existed a demand for more modern revolvers and the advantages they offered, such as accuracy, resistance to fouling, and speed in reloading. They also prevented the unnecessary waste of already manufactured firearms, and provided the average man with a more sophisticated sidearm that was less costly than a new Colt Peacemaker. The advantages and availability of converted cartridge revolvers in a variety of sizes and calibers contributed markedly to the westward expansion in the 1870s and the settling of the American frontier. It was an era filled with challenges and adventure, and it somehow seems appropriate that these legendary firearms became popular at this point in history.

Although firearms were a necessity on the frontier, many were also embellished with intricately detailed engraving. As documentation on these firearms became more available, it was possible to verify their authenticity and also create accurate reproductions.

Like the originals of the 1860s and 1870s, modern reproductions are also conversions of percussion revolvers, and are often built using the same methods and tools that gunsmiths used to convert them more than 130 years ago. A modern, custom-built conversion then becomes a handcrafted duplicate of an original design. These reproductions are collected by enthusiasts and used for props in films.

As more and more information about the history of cartridge conversion firearms became available, filmmakers realized that it was necessary to feature historically correct guns in their movies. In making a period film it is essential to take into account all aspects of the surroundings, such as buildings, clothing, and firearms. Because of the important role they played in American history, conversion firearms have been featured in several films and even used to help tell the story. For instance, in *Last Stand at Saber River* the 1860 Army conversion pistol relays the strife of Cable being gone for so long that the very guns used in the War Between the States had become almost obsolete by the time he returned home. As a focal point in the film the handcrafted Colt demonstrates both Cable's admiration for the workmanship and his need for a more modern firearm with which to protect his family and home. The advantage of the cartridge revolver against old-style percussion pistols is depicted several times throughout the film.

This is again portrayed in *Crossfire Trail* where an accurate reproduction of an 1872 Colt Open Top carried by the character Rafe Covington figures prominently in the opening scenes and throughout the film. In many ways, what would simply have been a prop in an older movie becomes an integral part of the story today.

Western films retell just a few of the events in American history, and as the props, including conversion firearms, become more accurate, that glimpse into the past also becomes more realistic for viewers. As a result, films have increased both the public interest in and the value of original Colt, Remington and other historic models, and *Metallic Cartridge Conversions* further underscores this phenomenon in contemporary filmmaking.

More importantly, however, I hope that both films and written information will primarily serve to remind us of what our American ancestors accomplished in an age before electricity and modern manufacturing. These legendary conversion firearms truly are the icons of an era of resolute strength and courage. They are as historic and important as the story of the American West itself.

Tom Selleck

Author Dennis Adler in period clothing by Classic Old West Styles and Wah Maker. The holsters and belt were custom made by Jim Barnard of Trailrider Products in Littleton, Colorado. Tom Selleck's 1860 Richards Type I revolver from the film *Last Stand at Saber River* is shown in the right-hand Miller-Fechet pattern holster, and a duplicate of the 1872 Open Top featured in *Crossfire Trail* is cradled in the 1872 Mexican-style double-loop Wolf Creek holster. Both guns were custom built by Kenny Howell of R&D Gunshop in Beloit, Wis.

Preface and Acknowledgments

When I hear someone describe me as an historian I often wonder to whom they are referring. Granted, my work is of an historical nature, but I am first and foremost an avowed firearms enthusiast.

Although I had been a gun collector for more than 30 years, it was not until I moved to Pennsylvania in 1993 that I was first exposed to the allure of black powder pistols while visiting Gettysburg. Shortly thereafter I purchased a Second Generation Colt 1851 Navy. I was fascinated both with the mechanics of the gun and its elegant design and construction. I then recalled, almost by coincidence, that Clint Eastwood had used similar pistols in several of his Westerns, *The Outlaw Josey Wales; The Good, The Bad, and the Ugly,* and a rather distinctive 1858 New Model Army Remington cartridge conversion in *Pale Rider.* I watched the films again and was even more captivated by these Colt and Remington revolvers. It was perhaps at that moment I became a "collector" and began the pursuit of original percussion revolvers, Colt Second Generation models, and custom-built cartridge conversions.

As an automotive historian and author, and yes, once again enthusiast, I came to realize that many of the automobile collectors with whom I worked on my books were also avid gun collectors whose interests frequently included early Colt and other percussion models built from the 1830s to the early 1870s. Through one such connection I met R. L. Wilson in 1997. Larry and I struck up an immediate friendship and it was his idea for me to write my first gun book

in 1998, *Colt Black Powder Reproductions & Replicas— A Collector's & Shooter's Guide.* Two other books followed—the *First* and *Second Editions* of the *Blue Book of Modern Black Powder Values.* All three were published by my friend Steve Fjestad, of Blue Book Publications, who was also one of Larry Wilson's numerous publishers.

My segue from cap-and-ball revolvers to cartridge conversions came during the debut of *Colt Blackpowder* at the 1998 Antique Arms Show in Las Vegas. It was there that I met another great friend, Bob Millington, a Colorado gunsmith with a talent for building remarkably accurate reproductions of Colt and Remington cartridge conversions. When I first saw Bob's display, I thought they were all original guns, as did many others. A new passion was born, and once again I jumped in with both feet. I commissioned Bob to build an authentic 1858 Remington conversion, c.1869. Several months later, while working on another automotive book, I traveled to Denver to pick up my gun. When I walked into Bob's shop there were three Remingtons on his workbench. I asked which was mine and he replied, "The one in the middle, the other two are originals." That was the start of a relationship that has resulted in eight authentic Colt and Remington cartridge conversions, all of which are featured in this book.

The search for knowledge led me to the same place I had been in 1997, at Larry Wilson's doorstep, asking why there wasn't a full-color history of the original guns and reproductions. And once again he presented me with the same challenge. "Why don't you write one?" So here we are, several years and many hundreds of photographs later.

In the process of writing and photographing this book I met many wonderful collectors who were willing to share both their guns and their knowledge with me. Among the numerous original Colt and Remington conversions pictured in this book are examples from four outstanding collections: the Dow and Russelle Heard Collection, J. D. Hofer Collection, Calvin Patrick Collection, and Roger Muckerheide Collection. They are all members of the Texas Gun Collectors Association, as is Bobby Vance, who owns the spectacular Thuer 1860 Army cartridge conversion with shoulder stock featured on the cover. You can't image the trust these guys had in me to ship their valued treasures to my studio in Pennsylvania for photography. Another collector and friend is Larry Compeau, who has a particular passion for Lefaucheux pinfire revolvers. He graciously supplied photos of these unique Civil War-era metallic cartridge pistols, along with a wealth of historic information. Saying, "thank you" falls well short of my deep appreciation and respect for these wonderful collectors.

As with any historical book, there is a great deal of research involved, and there is one individual who certainly paved the way for anyone writing about cartridge conversions, the late R. Bruce McDowell. His highly detailed accounting of Colt and Remington conversions, published in 1997 by Krause Publications, is a necessary reference for any collector of Remington and Colt cartridge revolvers, as is a new work on the history of Colt pocket pistols by John D. Breslin, William Q. Pirie, and David E. Price.

There are many people who become friends because of a shared hobby or interest, and among the many I have met over the years is one individual who never fails to produce remarkable Colt reproductions, Kenny Howell of R&D Gunshop. Kenny is best known for the guns he has built for Tom Selleck's epic westerns, several of which are pictured in this book. Kenny also introduced me to Tom Selleck.

All of this serves to underscore the camaraderie that exists among gun collectors, whose enthusiasm for preserving these historic arms goes far beyond just collecting. Each is an historian and antiquarian charged, for their brief time, with the responsibility of caring for these rare and magnificent creations. When you think about it, we are all just passing through, the guns were here before us and they will be here long after we are gone.

It is my hope that this book will help to perpetuate and further the appreciation and preservation of the original cartridge conversion firearms produced during the post-Civil War era and throughout the settling of the American West, as well as the fine selection of contemporary reproductions available today.

This book encompasses a very brief period, from the late 1860s to the early 1880s. During that time thousands of Colts, Remingtons, and other percussion revolvers were converted to fire metallic cartridges as a new era in the history of the gun began to unfold.

That story begins here, in the past.

Dennis Adler

The evolution of the pistol is depicted in five stages. It begins with the wheel-lock pistol c.1580, which was succeeded over the next three centuries by the flintlock c.1770, percussion lock c.1830, Samuel Colt's Paterson revolver c.1840, and the Colt 1860 Army Richards Type 1 metallic cartridge conversion revolver c.1871. All five examples shown are superb reproductions manufactured by some of the world's finest gunmakers.

CHAPTER 1

Evolution of the Pistol From Wheel-Locks to Wheel Guns

*I*t began with a problem. A matchlock rifle was difficult to carry, and for a cavalryman in the 16th century lighting a match wick on horseback and keeping it lit was easier said than done. Foot soldiers managed to engage in battle using matchlocks for more than a century, but the cavalry was still charging into combat with swords drawn. Of course, it took a lucky shot with a matchlock for a musketeer to hit almost anyone, let alone a moving horse and rider. And, a soldier wielding a heavy matchlock muzzleloader and weighed down with cast lead balls and pouches of gunpowder strung around his chest, was just as likely to kill himself with the lighted match as he was his intended target. There had to be a better way.

Around 1517, notes firearms historian R. L. Wilson, the wheel-lock was first seen in southern Germany, and the cities of Nuremberg, Augsburg, Munich, and Dresden, along with neighboring countries, such as the Netherlands and Denmark.

Although a complex design, the wheel-lock offered one the ability to carry a loaded firearm on their person, primed and ready to discharge. Produced in a variety of calibers, the basic design, though improved over time, remained in use for more than a century.

The intricate mechanism consisted of a steel wheel with a serrated edge that protruded through the flash pan. The wheel was mounted to a square spindle, which passed through the lock plate and was attached by means of a short chain (usually of three links) to a powerful spring. The last link ended in a toggle, which fit into a hook at the end of the mainspring. The gun was "cocked" by winding the

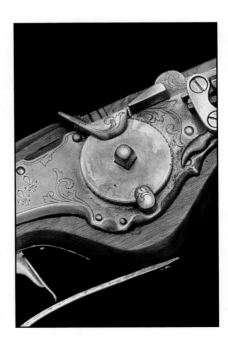

spindle with a spanner or key, placing the wheel under tension (held by the nose of the sear) and setting the trigger. It was very much like winding a clock. Once loaded and primed, the pan cover was closed and the jaws of the hammer (or cock) holding the pyrites set into position over the pan. In this

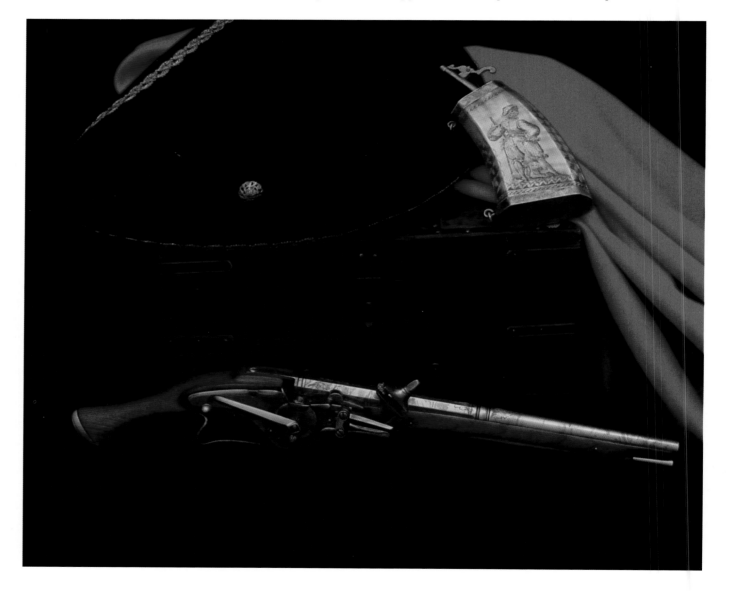

The wheel-lock mechanism, developed in Germany around 1517, provided the basis for the first practical pistols, which were seen in the latter half of the 16th century. The design of this example dates from the late 16th and early 17th century (1580-1600) and is one of a handful of superb reproductions that have been built in Quebec, Canada at Compagnie Royale D'Artillerie, under the supervision of firearms historian and manufacturer Guy Charlesvois. Valued at more than $3,000, the hand-built military-style pistol was later engraved in period motif by master gunsmith Phil Cravener, in Latrobe, Penn. Cravener also made the engraved 17th century powder flask. (Musketeer hat courtesy of Dirty Billys, Gettysburg, Pennsylvania)

The wheel-lock mechanism consisted of a steel wheel with a serrated edge that protruded through the flash pan. The wheel was mounted to a square spindle, which passed through the lock plate and was "cocked" by winding the spindle with a spanner or key, placing the wheel under tension and setting the trigger. Once loaded and primed, the pan cover was closed and the jaws of the hammer (or cock) holding the pyrites set into position over the pan.

posture the gun was now ready to fire. Pulling the trigger released the sear spring, causing the wheel to spin one revolution as the pan cover was thrown open. The spark created by the pyrites striking the serrated edge of the moving wheel ignited the priming mixture, which flashed through the touchhole and thus discharged the pistol. Needless to say, this was not an instantaneous ignition!

When the flintlock was perfected in the mid-17th century it brought the cost of pistol manufacturing down to the point where those of average means could afford to own one. The flintlock remained the dominant pistol design until the early 19th century. Pictured are three Pedersoli reproductions, a Queen Anne (c. 1680-1700), an America Remembers Washington & Lee Commemorative c.1776, a long-barreled Kentucky pistol—made popular on the frontier following the Revolutionary War—and a hand-built and embellished Kentucky pistol by Latrobe, Penn. custom gunmaker Phil Cravener.

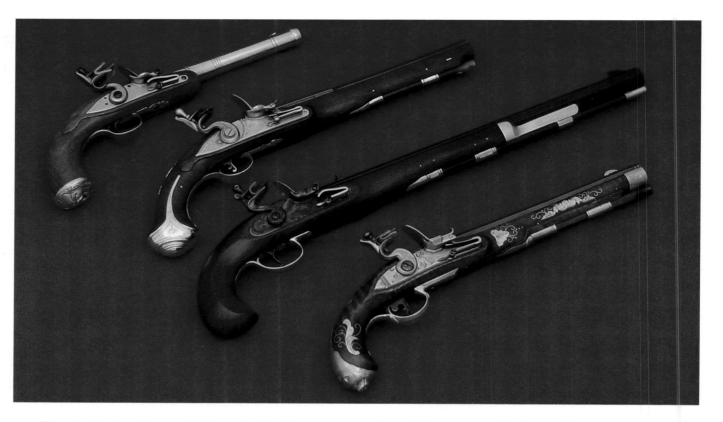

The greatest problem with the wheel-lock was reliability, not so much with the gun, as with the shooter. If, in the heat of battle, one wound the wheel in the wrong direction, the chain often broke or became dislodged, rendering the gun inoperable. And if one lost the spanner, there was no way in which to wind the mechanism—once more the gun was rendered useless, except as a rather elaborate truncheon.

Though the wheel-lock mechanism had the complexity of clockworks it was still vastly superior to the matchlock, if for no other reason than its adaptability as a small sidearm. By the late 16th century the pistol was born.

The wheel-lock pistol reigned supreme for more than 100 years, although mostly among the elite, until the flintlock succeeded it in the latter half of the 17th century. Sturdier, simpler to build, and far less costly to manufacture, the flintlock could be regarded as the firearms equivalent of Henry Ford's Model T, bringing the pistol within the reach of almost every man or woman. By the time of the American Revolution, the flintlock mechanism had become the standard of the world. Along with the trusty Pennsylvania longrifle

This is a rare c.1800-1840 swivel-barrel flintlock featuring iron furniture. Master gunsmith Leonard Day reproduced the early multiple-shot pistol design from an original gun. The swivel-barrel design was used on both rifles and pistols, allowing a quick follow-up shot by rotating the second barrel into battery. The pistol is shown with a reproduction map horn hand-carved by hornsmith Steven Shroyer.

19

(and similar designs), the flintlock pistol helped American patriots win their freedom. Firing one of these spectacular pistols today is another page right out of history.

The earliest flintlock designs appeared around 1615 but did not become widely accepted until the mid-17th century. The flintlock utilized a simpler, more robust firing mechanism actuated by the cock, which held a piece of flint between its jaws. Unlike the wheel-lock, which spun the serrated wheel to

The continuing evolution of the pistol saw the progression of the flintlock into the percussion lock in the early 19th century. Pictured are an engraved flintlock pistol and LePage percussion pistol. Italian gunmaker Davide Pedersoli handcrafted both reproductions.

create a spark, the flintlock hammer simply fell against a metal leaf called a frizzen, creating a spark with the flint that ignited the powder in the flash pan and thus the charge within the barrel. It was almost foolproof and far easier to operate. All one had to do was load it, prime the pan and, when ready, thumb back the hammer and pull the trigger.

The design proved quite versatile and there were many variations, including side-by-side double-barreled pistols, and innovative swivel-barrel examples, providing a quick follow-up shot by rotating a second barrel into battery. The firing mechanism could also be scaled down, allowing a diversity of pistol sizes from long-barreled, large-caliber examples to small pocket pistols easily concealed in a waistcoat. For nearly two centuries the flintlock remained unsurpassed until the Reverend Alexander Forsyth missed his dinner...quite literally.

An avid hunter and sportsman, Forsyth had grown frustrated with flintlocks, which while efficient, had a momentary delay from the ignition of the primer to the actual discharge of the firearm, often giving his prey sufficient warning to avoid becoming the evening's repast. Thus, the good Reverend began development of a more efficient means of igniting the powder charge, and in 1807 patented both the percussion lock and the fulminating mercury process used to ignite the powder charge. His idea, however, didn't exactly catch on. It would take more than a decade to perfect the percussion lock and improve the fulminating mercury process. The flintlock would maintain its popularity well into the early 19th century.

Historian Keith R. Dill, writing in the August 2000 issue of *Man at Arms* noted, "There is hard evidence to support the claim of only one gunmaker [as the inventor of the percussion cap] Joseph Egg. There are examples that may be dated to 1819, and documentary evidence indicating that he was probably producing the system a year before that. On the case labels that he used in the 1820s, the [London gunmaker] rightfully made claim of being *'the inventor of the copper cap.'*"

By the late 1820s the percussion era was ushered into the fullness of its development. In the end it was

R. L. Millington built this authentic reproduction of an original Colt 1860 Army Richards Type I conversion with 12-stop cylinder; one of the earliest of the C. B. Richards patented Colt cartridge conversions. An original is pictured elsewhere in this book.

all so simple, a copper cap containing the mercury fulminate (a gray, crystalline solid), was placed over a hollow tube and detonated by the impact of the hammer, producing a small flame that was sent directly into the powder charge causing almost instantaneous detonation. Taking the idea one step further was Samuel Colt's patent for the Paterson five-shot revolver in 1836 (with production beginning the following year in Paterson, New Jersey). The pistol had finally come of age.

Although the Paterson and Sam Colt's first firearms manufacturing enterprise both failed, his second attempt in 1847, built upon the shoulders of the now legendary Walker .44 caliber revolver made famous in the war with Mexico, launched both Colt's and America on the road to an industrial revolution within the firearms industry.

By the beginning of the American Civil War in 1861 the Colt's Patent Fire Arms Manufacturing Company had created an entire range of revolvers, from small-caliber pocket-sized pistols to the mighty .44 caliber Dragoons (successors to the 1847 Walker), and the highly regarded .36 caliber 1851 Navy and .44 caliber 1860 Army, the principal sidearms of the U.S. military throughout the Civil War.

Sam Colt may have perfected and patented the design for the revolving cylinder pistol, but he wasn't alone in the American firearms business; he was instead the catalyst for an emerging industry that flourished throughout the 19th century.

Among Colt's most successful contemporaries was E. Remington & Sons in Ilion, New York. After the Colt's patent for the revolving cylinder expired, Remington introduced the revolutionary 1858 New Model Army in .44 caliber and lighter .36 caliber Navy version. The Remington revolvers featured a solid top strap and a fixed (threaded) barrel, providing greater strength and ease of operation compared to Colt's wedge-pinned barrel and open-top design, which by 1858 was now almost 20 years old. One could change out a Remington cylinder in seconds, without having to remove the barrel. The top strap added strength to the frame, and above all else, the threaded Remington barrels assured greater accuracy. In the heat of battle, a Colt barrel wedged too tightly could easily bind the cylinder. Colt nevertheless remained the dominant American pistol of the Civil War era, and well into the postwar move west in the late 1860s and early 1870s. For more than 35 years the percussion revolver, either manufactured by Colt's, Remington, or others, both here and abroad, remained the dominant design.

By the late 1860s, the black powder pistol had come a long way from the primitive 16th century wheel-lock, but in many ways it had remained much the same for nearly 300 years, requiring three individual elements in order to function: powder, ball, and a means of igniting the charge. The advent of the metallic cartridge, which combined all three components into one, hastened the beginning of a new era in American firearms manufacturing.

As the American frontier opened up in the post-Civil War period, the cartridge pistol become a means by which one could afford self-protection through the concealment of a charged and readied sidearm. The pistol could be easily retrieved and in time of need was the great equalizer of both man and beast.

Beginning in 1847 Samuel Colt brought the percussion pistol into the fullness of its development. Colt's produced a wide variety of black powder revolvers between 1847 and 1873, which included the massive .44 caliber 1847 Walker (top left and going counter clockwise) .44 caliber First, Second and Third Model Dragoons, the five-shot. 36 caliber 1862 Pocket Police, .31 caliber 1848 Baby Dragoon, and .36 caliber 1862 Pocket Navy, .44 caliber 1860 Army with rebated cylinder or fluted cylinder, and the .36 caliber 1861 Navy, and 1851 Navy, the latter four becoming the principal sidearms of the Union forces during the Civil War.

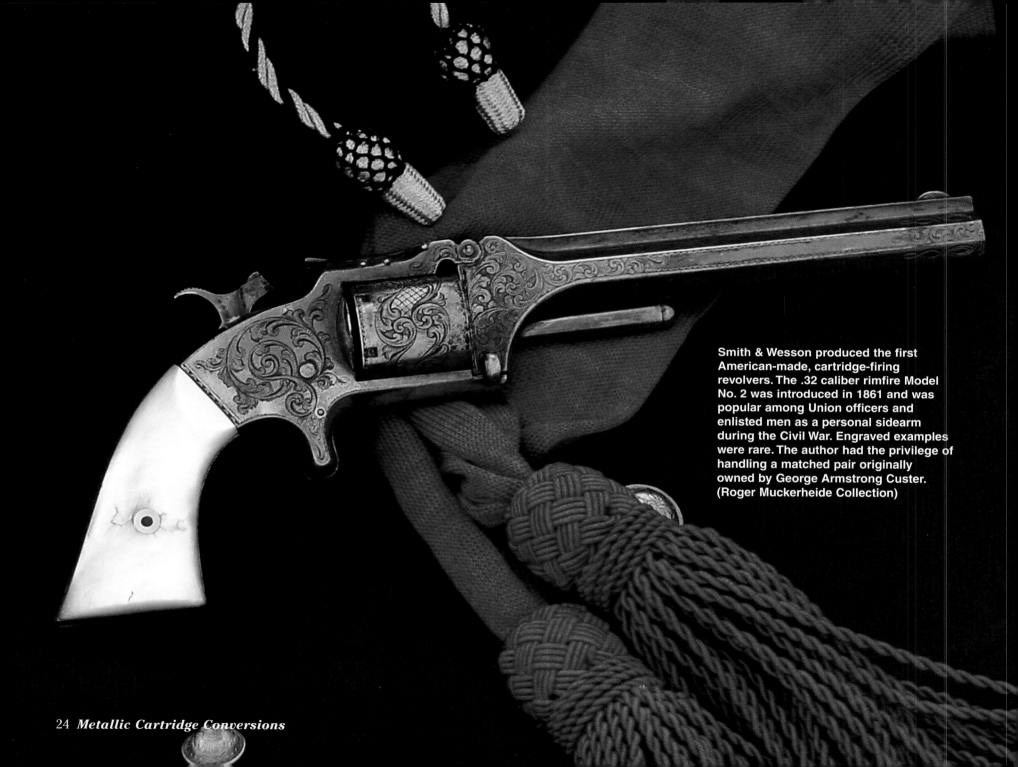

Smith & Wesson produced the first American-made, cartridge-firing revolvers. The .32 caliber rimfire Model No. 2 was introduced in 1861 and was popular among Union officers and enlisted men as a personal sidearm during the Civil War. Engraved examples were rare. The author had the privilege of handling a matched pair originally owned by George Armstrong Custer. (Roger Muckerheide Collection)

CHAPTER 2

Early Development of the Metallic Cartridge in Europe and the United States

The American Civil War—
A Mandate for Better Weapons

Although Colt and Remington percussion pistols were regarded as contemporary firearms in the United States, cartridge-firing revolvers had been in use throughout Europe since the 1840s. And the metallic cartridge itself was even older.

The first record dates back to 1812 when Swiss inventor Jean Samuel Pauley received a patent for a self-contained, self-primed, centerfire metallic cartridge. Four years earlier Pauley had applied for another patent, this covering the design for the first in-line rifle, which he improved upon in 1812 with the introduction of a breechloader. A gunmaker named Johann Niklaus von Dreyse, who apprenticed under Pauley from 1808 to 1814, further improved the in-line concept with his 1838 patent for the turnbolt rifle, which evolved into the well-known Prussian

Needlegun a decade later. It was this design upon which German gunmaker Paul Mauser based his celebrated Model 1868 turnbolt cartridge rifle. The pioneering Mauser design was adopted by the German military in 1871, and provided the foundation for the celebrated 1903 Springfield.

By the mid 1840s rimfire cartridges were in common use throughout Europe and in 1854 the first centerfire or central fire rounds were produced. However, in 1843 a third type of bullet had been invented in France by gunmaker Casimir Lefaucheux (pronounced *lue-foe-SHOW*), and it had become exceedingly popular in Europe and the United States by the 1860s. It was known as the Lefaucheux pinfire, which literally meant that a firing pin was contained within each individual bullet! The operation was quite clever. The hammer fell on a cartridge pin

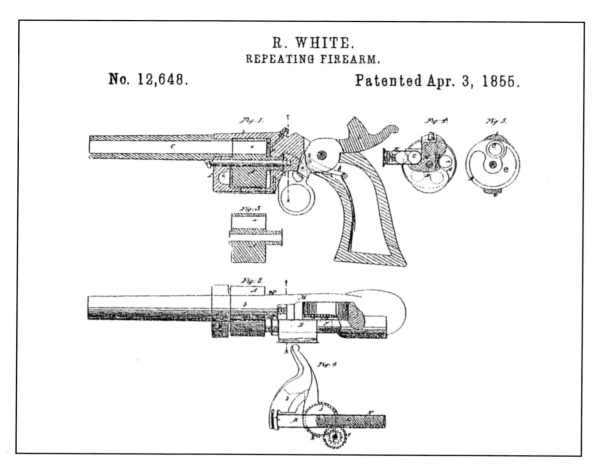

Inventor Rollin White was originally a Colt employee, however, when he approached Samuel Colt with the idea for the bored-through cylinder Colt showed little interest. White received a patent for his invention on April 3, 1855 and on November 17, 1856 he signed an agreement with Horace Smith and Daniel B. Wesson granting S&W an exclusive license to use bored-through cylinders in its products. (Photo courtesy R. L. Wilson)

extending above the rim of the cylinder through a notch, the pin in turn struck a percussion cap inside the chambered round, igniting the powder. While very effective, each Lefaucheux bullet was a very *live* round and it was in one's best interest never to fumble or drop a pinfire cartridge!

Lefaucheux's son Eugene was the first to adapt the pinfire cartridge to a revolver and his French patent (April 15, 1854) for the bored-through cylinder

preceded Rollin White's by a full year. The Lefaucheux revolver was a superior design to the contemporary cap-and-ball percussion arms being used by the American military in the 1860s, and was often preferred by both Union and Confederate troops. In Europe the Lefaucheux pistol had been adopted by the French Navy in 1858, Sweden and Spain followed suit in 1863 and Norway in 1864.

The mandate for better arms during the Civil War led President Abraham Lincoln to commission Marcellus Hartley, a partner in the New York firearms importing firm of Schuyler, Hartley & Graham Co. to supply the Union Army with French Lefaucheux pistols and pinfire ammunition in 1862. The Union Army received 1,900 Lefaucheux pinfire revolvers through Hartley and purchased another 10,000 under direct contract during the war. The Confederacy was also purchasing Lefaucheux revolvers along with a small number of percussion LeMat revolvers, also produced in France and refitted to chamber pinfire cartridges. From 1861 to 1865 the Confederate States of America purchased as many as 2,500 Lefaucheux revolvers, which became the fourth most commonly used sidearm throughout the Civil War, surpassed only by the Colt, Remington, and Starr percussion pistols. Between the North and South more than 1,000,000 pinfire cartridges were also ordered during the conflict, the largest single requisition for metallic cartridges throughout the Civil War.

Marcellus Hartley handled the majority of Union requisitions for Lefaucheux revolvers and pinfire cartridges. A key figure in the American firearms industry of the 1860s (importing pinfire arms and

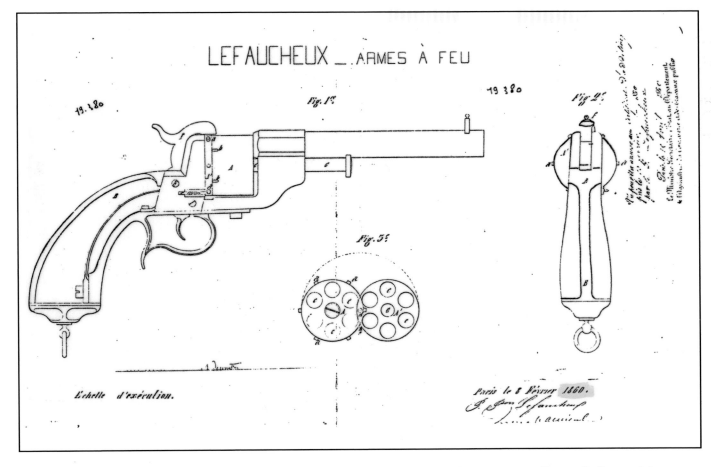

LEFAUCHEUX _ ARMES À FEU

Échelle d'exécution.

Paris le 8 Février 1860.

Eugene Lefaucheux was the first to adapt the pinfire cartridge invented by his father Casimir, to fit a revolver. His French patent (April 15, 1854) for the bored-through cylinder preceded Rollin White's by one year. The Lefaucheux revolver was a superior design to the contemporary cap-and-ball percussion arms being used by the American military, and the U.S. Army requisitioned more than 10,000 during the Civil War. (Patent reproduced from *The Pinfire System* with the permission of Chris Curtis)

ammunition before, during, and after the war), he was also responsible for establishing the Union Metallic Cartridge Co., which was one of only three American firms known to have manufactured and marketed pinfire ammunition in any quantity. Because of the availability of ammunition in America, the Lefaucheux and other pinfire revolvers were used longer and more extensively by Union forces than in the Southern armies. [1]

The First American Pistol Cartridge

As the 11 Southern States were seceding from the Union, (1860-61) Daniel B. Wesson (of Smith & Wesson) was perfecting a self-contained, .22 caliber rimfire metallic cartridge (essentially the same .22 caliber short rimfire bullet still used today), for which S&W received a patent in 1860. Wesson and his partner Horace Smith had also wisely acquired the

The Lefaucheux pistol was often preferred by both Union and Confederate troops. The design allowed for easy loading by opening the gate at the back of the recoil shield, and the ejector was attached to the frame. The small slot at the rear of each chamber is where the pin extended above the edge of the cylinder. The hammer fell directly on top of the cylinder striking the pin and discharging the cartridge. The caliber was 12mm, slightly larger than today's 9mm cartridges. (Gun and holster courtesy The Horse Soldier, Gettysburg, Penn.)

exclusive rights to the 1855 Rollin White patent covering the manufacture of a bored-through cylinder, a design in which Samuel Colt had shown little interest when White (a former Colt employee) first presented it to him. With the White patent S&W had an out-and-out monopoly within the American firearms industry until 1869.

When the extension on Colt's patent for a revolving mechanism expired, Smith & Wesson quickly introduced their first cartridge-firing revolver in January 1857. The S&W Model No. 1 was a 7-shot, .22 caliber rimfire pocket pistol. An improved Second Issue model was introduced in 1860, by which time S&W had sold more than 11,000 cartridge revolvers.

The Smith & Wesson revolvers became extremely popular during the Civil War, however their small caliber prevented them from being approved for military use by the U.S. Army Ordnance Department, even though S&W had added a larger six-shot, .32 caliber version, the Model No. 2, in 1861. The medium-frame Model No. 2, with either a 5- or 6-inch barrel, was in such demand throughout the war that the factory had a three-year backlog of orders! Officers and infantrymen frequently carried the No. 2 as a back-up pistol. Between 1861 and 1874 a total of 77,155 were built.

The considerable number of cartridge-firing revolvers used by both sides during the Civil War contributed to a number of patent infringements involving Smith & Wesson and Rollin White. The White patent, however, could not restrict the import of European cartridge-firing firearms, thus French, British and Belgian manufacturers produced the majority of cartridge pistols seen in America between 1861 and 1871.

New Orleans physician Dr. Jean Alexandre Francois LeMat, who had moved to the United States from France in 1843, designed the LeMat percussion revolver. Developed prior to the Civil War, the large nine-shot pistol (with a grapeshot barrel underneath) was produced for the Confederate Army in Liège, Paris, and London between 1862 and 1865. Approximately 3,000 were built, a portion of which were converted in France to accept the pinfire cartridge. (Photos by Terry Tremewan from the Larry Compeau collection)

Here is a rather ominous view of a 10-shot Lefaucheux revolver. The large loading gate opened at the top right (small tab) and allowed for the easy ejection of spent cartridges and rapid loading. The ejector can be seen attached to the frame and directly in front of the top chamber. (Photo by Terry Tremewan from the Larry Compeau collection)

The most common infringements of the White patent were for small-caliber revolvers similar in appearance to the S&W Model No. 1 and Model No 2; the most well-known of which were the .22 caliber Fourth Model pocket pistols manufactured by Allen & Wheelock in Worchester, Mass., a variety of small-caliber pocket models developed by Bacon Arms Co. in Norwich, Connecticut, the rather prolific and

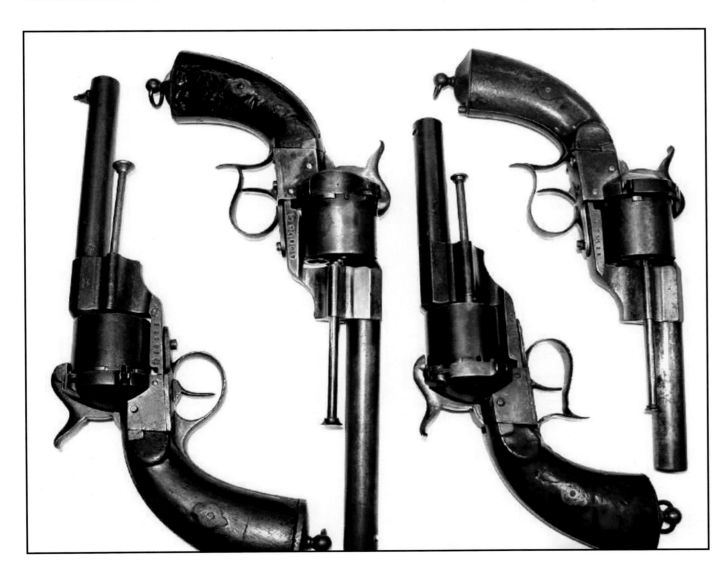

The Lefaucheux pistol was produced in a number of variations. The examples pictured are chambered for 12mm pinfire cartridges. (Photo by Terry Tremewan from the Larry Compeau collection)

blatantly copied S&W-style, spur-trigger, tip-up models produced by Manhattan Fire Arms Manufacturing Co. of Newark, New Jersey, and the .32 caliber S.A. Belt and Pocket Pistols built by Lucius W. Pond of Worchester, Mass. There were, however, many similar designs throughout the early 1860s produced briefly by American manufactures like F. D. Bliss (1863-1864), Gross Arms Co. (1864-1866), E. A. Prescott (1861-1863), James Reid (1861-1865), Springfield Arms Co. (1863), and Wm. Uhlinger (1861-1865). [2]

The most advanced of all American cartridge revolvers was the Moore .32 caliber rimfire model, an original and unique design that had the misfortune of firing metallic cartridges loaded at the breech, which constituted an infringement of the Rollin White patent.

The Moore's Patent Firearms Co. of Brooklyn, New York, introduced its Single Action Belt Revolver in 1861 but the following year lost a patent infringement

The Lefaucheux pinfire was an interesting alternative to the early rimfire and centerfire metallic cartridge. The pin is clearly shown on this 12mm round. When struck by the hammer, the pin hit the percussion cap within the cartridge igniting the powder. (Photo by Terry Tremewan from the Larry Compeau collection)

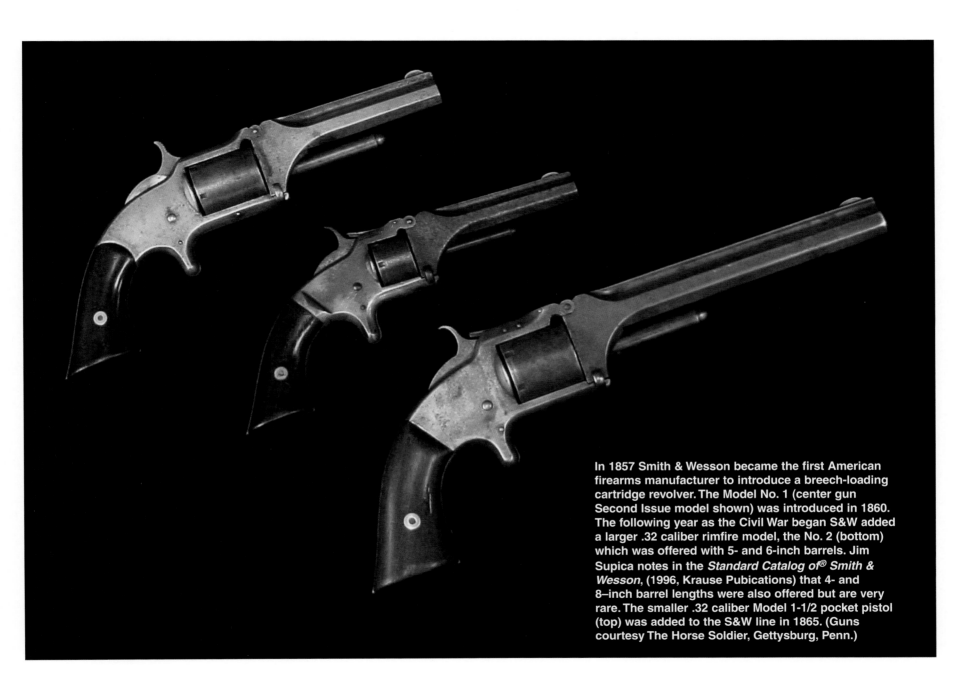

In 1857 Smith & Wesson became the first American firearms manufacturer to introduce a breech-loading cartridge revolver. The Model No. 1 (center gun Second Issue model shown) was introduced in 1860. The following year as the Civil War began S&W added a larger .32 caliber rimfire model, the No. 2 (bottom) which was offered with 5- and 6-inch barrels. Jim Supica notes in the *Standard Catalog of® Smith & Wesson*, (1996, Krause Pubications) that 4- and 8–inch barrel lengths were also offered but are very rare. The smaller .32 caliber Model 1-1/2 pocket pistol (top) was added to the S&W line in 1865. (Guns courtesy The Horse Soldier, Gettysburg, Penn.)

This rare Louis D. Nimschke engraved S&W Model No. 2 is fitted with pearl stocks. Note the original ammo box of .32 caliber rimfire cartridges. Wild Bill Hickok was carrying a Model No. 2 the day he was murdered in Deadwood, South Dakota. [5] (Roger Muckerheide Collection)

Deluxe embellishment by Louis D. Nimschke, the chief engraver for Schuyler, Hartley and Graham of New York City, was a hallmark of many Smith & Wesson and Colt revolvers produced from the 1850s up until 1900.

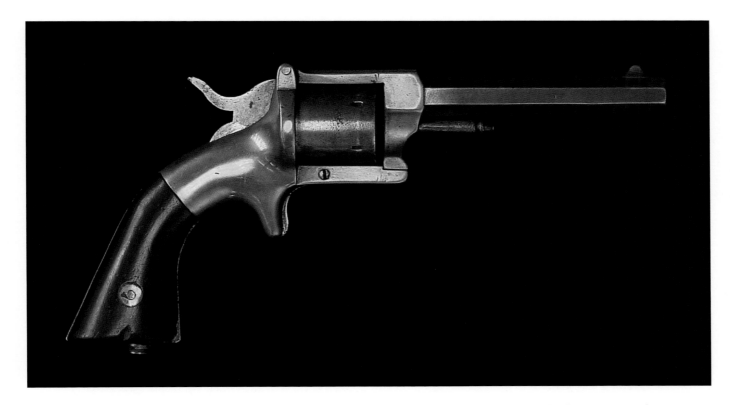

Lucius W. Pond was one of many American gunmakers who decided to test the Rollin White patent in 1861. The .32 caliber Pond single action pocket (pictured) and belt models were produced until 1862. After failing in a patent infringement battle with S&W, Pond sold the remaining inventory of 4,486 guns to S&W. The revolvers were then marked MANUF'D FOR SMITH & WESSON PAT'D. (Gun courtesy The Horse Solider, Gettysburg, Penn.)

suit with Smith & Wesson and Rollin White. In 1862 they had brought their case before the court against manufacturers (Manhattan in particular) and distributors of Smith & Wesson copies and firearms utilizing a bored-through cylinder to fire metallic cartridges. S&W then agreed to buy outright the inventories of several companies that had lost the court battle, among them Daniel Moore, who sold S&W 3,299 of his S.A. Belt Revolvers in 1863. The last examples built were marked MF'D FOR SMITH & WESSON. Another 4,880 revolvers were purchased from Lucius W. Pond; 1,437 from James Warner; and 1,124 from Bacon Manufacturing Co. [3]

The best however was the Moore, a medium-frame, seven-shot revolver with a swing-out cylinder and barrel combination. A lever at the back of the recoil shield released the mechanism allowing both the cylinder and barrel to pivot to the right, clearing the recoil shield and permitting the loading and unloading of each chamber. The latter facilitated by a hand-held extractor rod stored under the barrel (similar to old flintlock pistol rammers). Given the period, this was a well conceived and efficient means of eliminating the loading and unloading problems associated with early cartridge-firing revolvers. Although limited in production, the Moore became a popular sidearm among Union troops.

Rollin White, the man who held the patent for the breech-loading, bored-through cylinder, also produced a revolver beginning in 1861, which happened to closely resemble the S&W Model No. 1. Built in Lowell, Mass., the seven-shot, .22 caliber pocket pistols were marked MADE FOR SMITH & WESSON. BY ROLLIN WHITE ARMS CO. LOWELL MASS. The cylinders were stamped with both the White patent date and White pistol patent date, PATENTED APRIL 3. 1855 DEC. 18. 1860.

Despite the prolific number of cartridge-firing revolvers imported from Europe and manufactured in the United States by Smith & Wesson and its various imitators, throughout the Civil War the loose-powder,

patch, cap-and-ball percussion revolver remained the dominant sidearm of the Union and Confederate forces as well as the majority of civilians on both sides of the conflict. By 1868, however, the true heirs were about to set foot upon the stage as the Rollin White patent neared the end of its 14-year duration.

Colt's and Remington had been marking time for more than a decade, neither willing to challenge S&W and White. Following Samuel Colt's precedent with the revolving cylinder, White had applied for a patent extension in 1868 but the Commissioner of Patents had refused his request. White then appealed to Congress which drafted a Bill (S-273) "An act for the relief of Rollin White" that passed both houses but was returned unsigned by President Ulysses S.

Another make that fell under the S&W and Rollin White patent was the Prescott, which again was quite different in design from the Smith & Wesson models, but still subject to the infringement suit. Produced by E. A. Prescott of Worchester, Mass. from 1861 to 1863, the six-shot, medium-frame revolver was chambered for .38 caliber rimfire making it a more potent weapon. Both iron- and brass-frame models were usually fitted with a 7-1/2-inch octagonal barrel. Only a few hundred were produced before the S&W suit halted manufacturing. (Gun courtesy The Horse Solider,

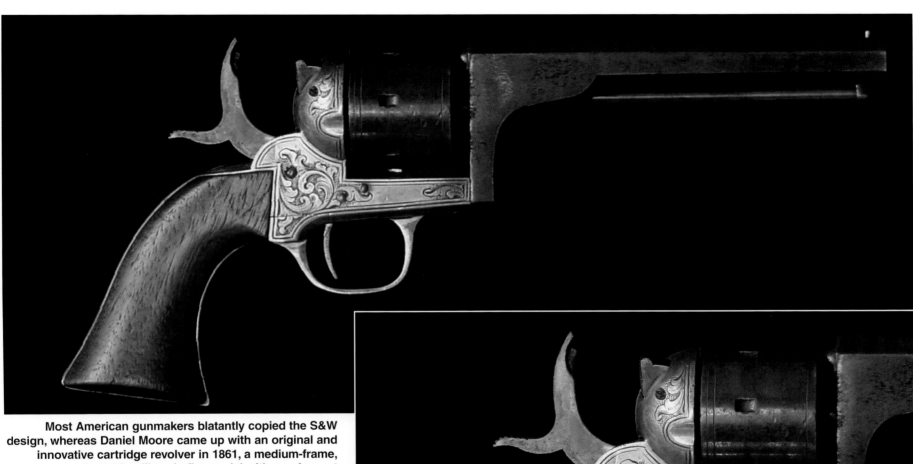

Most American gunmakers blatantly copied the S&W design, whereas Daniel Moore came up with an original and innovative cartridge revolver in 1861, a medium-frame, seven-shot, .32 caliber rimfire model with a swing-out cylinder and barrel combination. A lever at the back of the recoil shield released the mechanism allowing both the cylinder and barrel to pivot to the right, clearing the recoil shield and permitting the loading and unloading of each chamber. A hand-held ejector rod was stored under the barrel (similar to old flintlock pistol rammers). After losing a patent infringement suit with S&W Moore sold them 3,299 of his revolvers in 1863. The last examples built were marked MF'D FOR SMITH & WESSON. Quite a few were purchased by Union officers during the Civil War. (Gun courtesy The Horse Solider, Gettysburg, Penn.)

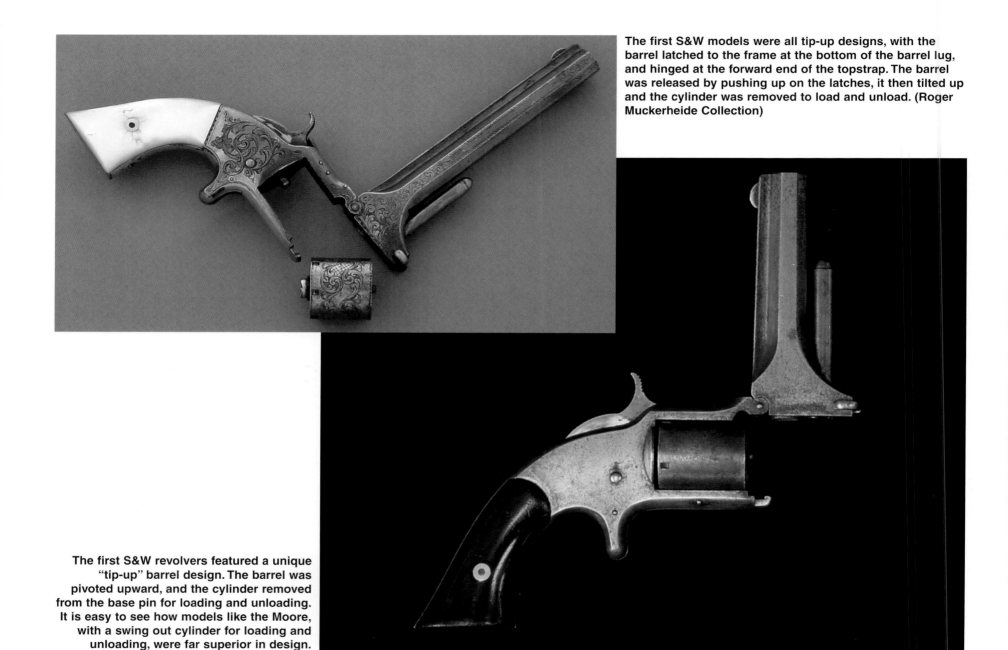

The first S&W models were all tip-up designs, with the barrel latched to the frame at the bottom of the barrel lug, and hinged at the forward end of the topstrap. The barrel was released by pushing up on the latches, it then tilted up and the cylinder was removed to load and unload. (Roger Muckerheide Collection)

The first S&W revolvers featured a unique "tip-up" barrel design. The barrel was pivoted upward, and the cylinder removed from the base pin for loading and unloading. It is easy to see how models like the Moore, with a swing out cylinder for loading and unloading, were far superior in design.

Grant.[4] White's failure to get an extension opened the floodgates for the development of both the metallic cartridge and breech-loading revolver. Colt's and Remington were about to add a new chapter to the story of the handgun.

[1] The *Pinfire System* by Gene Smith and Chris Curtis, 1981, Gene Smith Publications.
[2] *Flayderman's Guide to Antique American Firearms*, 7th Edition, by Norm Flayderman, 1998, Krause Publications.
[3] *A Study of Colt Conversions and Other Percussion Revolvers* by R. Bruce McDowell, 1997, Krause Publications.
[4] Ibid
[5] *They Callled Him Wild Bill* by Joseph G. Rosa

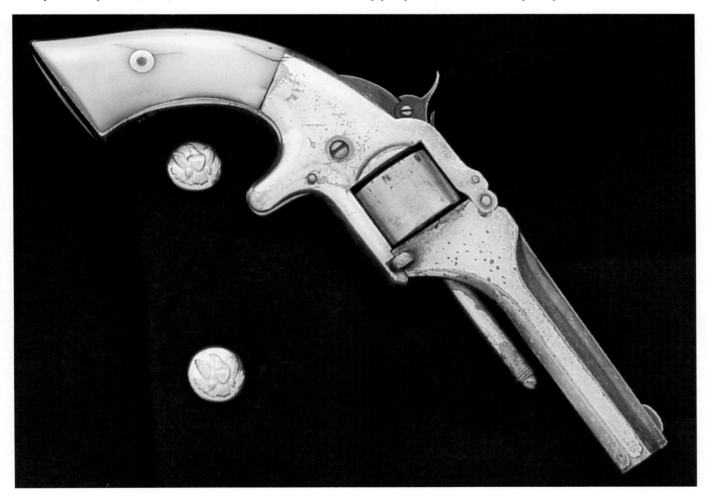

Here is a First Issue S&W No. 1 .22 caliber rimfire revolver with ivory stocks and nickel finish. The seven-shot No.1 made an ideal pocket revolver. The First Issue models are distinguished by their rounded frame, which follows into the grip strap. Later versions, known as the Second Issue revolver had flat sides and a distinctive rim above the grips. (Roger Muckerheide Collection)

Colt's entry into the breech-loading metallic cartridge conversion era was three years behind Remington, but when Hartford finally introduced the Richards Type I conversion for the 1860 Army it was an immediate success. This early example is pictured with an original box of Frankford Arsenal .44 caliber cartridges. The Frankford Arsenal in Pennsylvania was the principal supplier of metallic cartridges to the U.S. military. (Dow and Russelle Heard Collection)

12 "Martin" Cartridges
for
Colt's & Remington's Army Revolvers.
Calibre .44.
Powder: 30 grains. Bullet, 225 grains.
FRANKFORD ARSENAL, PA.,
APRIL 1, 1874.
Patented March 25, 1869, February 14, 1871.

CHAPTER 3

Patent vs. Patent

Colt, Remington, Smith & Wesson, and Rollin White

S amuel Colt had no idea what he had done when he turned down Rollin White's offer for the patent rights to the bored-through cylinder, nor would he ever. Colt died on January 10, 1862, never to know the outcome of the Civil War, or the importance of the metallic cartridge. The Colt's Patent Fire Arms Manufacturing Company, however, would suffer the consequences of his decision long after the conflict had ended.

Following the Civil War, Colt's and Remington found themselves with an abundance of surplus cap-and-ball revolvers, Colt's in particular, having been the primary supplier of arms to the U.S. military.

As firearms technology advanced from the cap-and-ball revolver to the beginning of the metallic cartridge era in the late 1860s, this precipitated a need to move inventories of percussion arms that

were fast becoming obsolete. It was only now that Sam Colt's unfortunate decision began to weigh in.

Historian R. L. Wilson notes that two seminal events led to the advent of the metallic cartridge revolver in America. "First, was the expiration of the Colt's patent for the mechanically revolved cylinder, which had prevented any other American gun manufacturer from producing revolvers until 1857. Second was the 1855 Rollin White patent for the bored-through, breech-loading cylinder, acquired through exclusive license by Smith & Wesson in November 1856."

When the Colt's patent expired, Smith & Wesson, Remington, and other American manufacturers immediately began producing revolvers, however, no one but Smith & Wesson and Rollin White could legally manufacture cartridge-firing revolvers utilizing

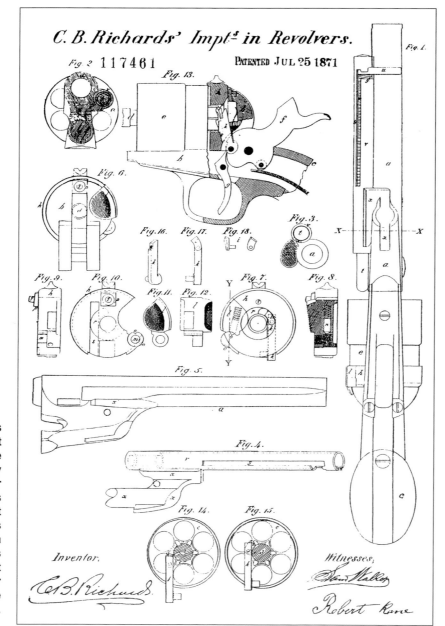

The C. B. Richards patent for the Colt 1860 Army cartridge conversion dated July 25, 1871. Inventor Charles B. Richards was a prominent Colt employee who was responsible for a number of designs including the Colt Open Top, Clover Leaf, and New Line pocket pistols.

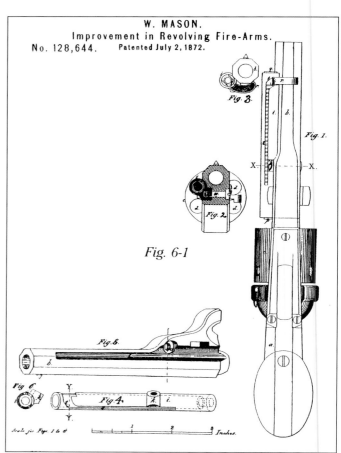

Following the Richards Type II design, which switched from a breech ring-mounted rebounding firing pin, to a hammer-mounted firing pin, William Mason designed a new and less costly means of attaching the ejector assembly to the barrel

Having agreed to pay a $1 per gun royalty to S&W, Remington was licensed to produce a cartridge conversion revolver in 1868, a year before the expiration of the Rollin White patent. The earliest models built on the 1858 Army, were converted to fire five .46 caliber rimfire cartridges. These early models did not have ejectors. As part of the agreement with S&W it was required that the Rollin White patent date be stamped on all Remington conversion cylinders. (J. D. Hofer Collection)

a breech-loading, bored-through cylinder. Thus as one hand was untied, the other was bound.

The various attempts during the Civil War to sidestep the patent were quickly thwarted by S&W and White who, as pointed out in the previous chapter, aggressively pursued all violators. As a

result, the design and development of cartridge-firing revolvers produced in America up until 1869 was fraught with legal battles over patent infringements, thereby stifling the progress of the metallic cartridge for more than a decade. This of course, begs the question, "Why didn't Smith & Wesson make

The Colt 1860 Army (top) was an ideal candidate for conversion because of its sturdy design. The re-machining of the barrel to accept the ejector assembly, however, was a costly process, which prompted the adoption of the less complicated William Mason design in 1872. (Dennis Russell Collection)

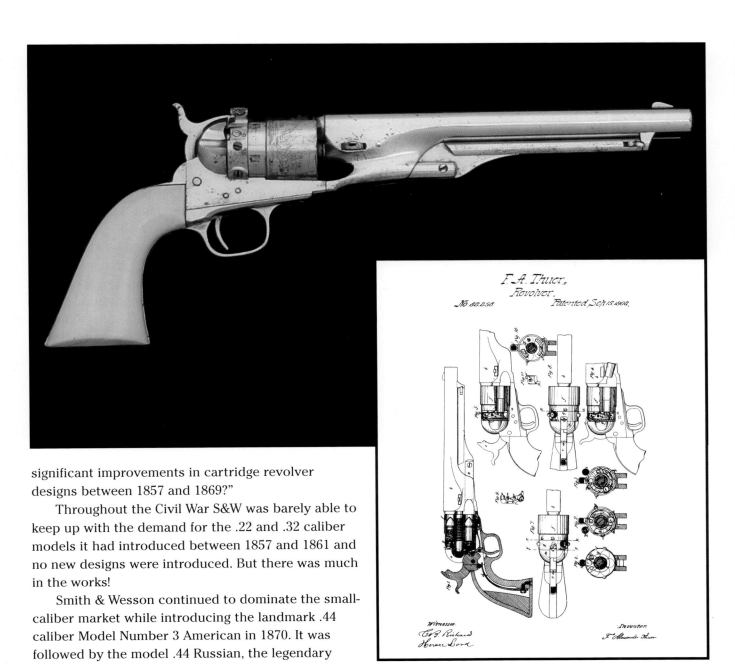

Colt's management had decided not to challenge the S&W and Rollin White patent, which had been vigorously enforced since 1861, however, in an effort to compete within the emerging metallic cartridge market, Colt's introduced the Thuer in September 1868. Originally based on the 1860 Army, the standard percussion cylinder was removed and replaced by a breechplate and new cylinder. The bullets were then inserted in conventional cap-and-ball fashion and pressed into each chamber with the loading lever. (Roger Muckerheide Collection)

F. A. Thuer.
Revolver.
No 82.258   Patented Sep.15.1868.

Witnesses   Inventor
Co B. Richard   F. Alexander Thuer
Horace Lord

significant improvements in cartridge revolver designs between 1857 and 1869?"

Throughout the Civil War S&W was barely able to keep up with the demand for the .22 and .32 caliber models it had introduced between 1857 and 1861 and no new designs were introduced. But there was much in the works!

Smith & Wesson continued to dominate the small-caliber market while introducing the landmark .44 caliber Model Number 3 American in 1870. It was followed by the model .44 Russian, the legendary

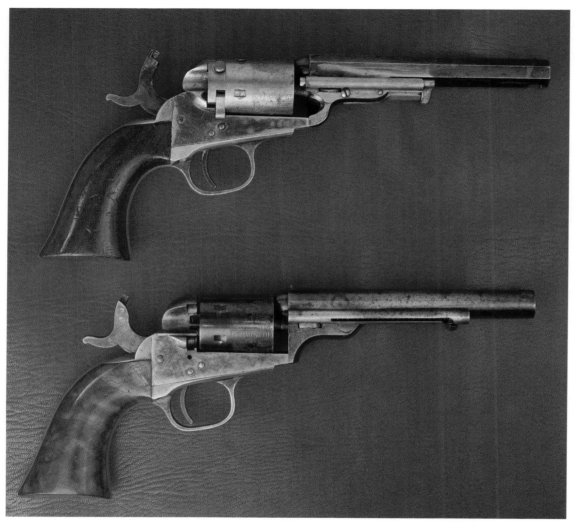

Colt's experimental department was at work on cartridge conversion designs before the White patent expired. Pictured are predecessors to the first production models introduced in 1871, an experimental 1851 Navy (top) and an 1871-72 Open Top. Both designs utilized a deeply channeled recoil shield, the Navy was fitted with an experimental loading gate and ejector assembly. John R. Hegeman Jr. formerly owned both examples. (Photo courtesy R. L. Wilson)

Schofield, and improved New Model Number 3, all of which featured S&W's pioneering top-break design and automatic cartridge ejector.

For Colt's, the period from 1855 to 1869 was an interesting turn of events. The Hartford, Conn. Arms maker was now the one on the receiving end of an unbreakable patent. Just as Samuel Colt had prevented any American company from manufacturing revolvers until his patent expired, Smith & Wesson, and E. Remington & Sons (through a licensing agreement providing S&W with a $1 royalty per gun), were the only U.S. manufacturers legally permitted to build a breech-loading, cartridge-firing revolver, and Remington wasn't granted rights until 1868. Aside from the somewhat Machiavellian approach taken in 1868 by F. Alexander Thuer and Colt's to circumvent the legal limitations of the Rollin White patent, Colt's was forced to wait, and did not introduce a breech-loading model until 1871.

The Thuer design did not use a bored-through cylinder. Each cartridge was loaded from the front of the cylinder using the rammer, as one would have loaded a round or conical lead ball. A similar approach was taken by Pond, after losing a patent infringement suit with S&W in 1862. The .22 and .32 caliber rimfire Pond revolver utilized chamber tubes, which were loaded with the bullet and inserted into the cylinder. There were a number of .22 and .32 caliber variations built on the front-loading principal during the 1860s, however, only Colt's managed to offer a large caliber model, the Thuer Army was a .44.

While Colt's is often attributed with producing the first cartridge conversions, Remington's licensing agreement under the auspices of the U.S. Army

Metallic cartridges for Colts (and Remingtons) were produced by a number of manufacturers including the Winchester Repeating Arms Company, the United States Cartridge Company, the Frankford Arsenal in Pennsylvania, and The Union Metallic Cartridge Company, which was founded by Marcellus Hartley, a partner in the New York firearms importing firm of Schuyler, Hartley & Graham Co. (Dow and Russelle Heard Collection)

Ordnance Department allowed the New York arms maker to precede Colt's in the production of breech-loading conversions. This was a significant head start, and when one considers the superior design of the Remington revolver, the advantage in the early post-Civil War years was certainly held by Remington.

While Colt's biggest competitor was producing the first large-caliber cartridge conversion revolvers in 1868, the Hartford arms maker was busy developing its own designs. The Thuer patent was dated September 15, 1868. The C.B. Richards patent for Colt's 1860 Army, utilizing a breechplate with an internal rebounding firing pin, and a complete ejector assembly fitted to the rammer channel, was granted on July 25, 1871. This became the first production breech-loading cartridge conversion model offered by Colt's.

At the same time, Colt's introduced the 1871-72 Open Top revolvers, the first all-new cartridge-firing models to bear the Colt name. Designed by C. B. Richards and William Mason, the Open Tops were based on the 1860 Army frame but fitted with all-new barrels and cylinders.

In 1872 the William Mason patent for Colt's, "Improvements in Revolving Fire-Arms," was adopted and made available on a wide variety of percussion models, including the 1851 Navy and Colt's 1862 pocket pistols. However, as Wilson so poignantly notes in *The Book of Colt Firearms*, "Progress from the earliest experiments through the last proceeded so quickly that the Open Top .44 revolvers themselves were obsolete almost as soon as their total number of approximately 7,000 had been completed."

The final evolution came with the introduction of the 1873 Colt Single Action Army, commonly known as the Peacemaker. Interestingly, this is not where the story of black powder cartridge conversions ends— this is where it begins.

With thousands of surplus Colt and Remington cap-and-ball revolvers and parts on hand, Colt's began converting many of its own guns, first to the Thuer, then Richards, and later Richards-Mason designs. Cartridge conversions were far more affordable than the new Peacemaker, less than half

the price, and Colt's would convert a customer's percussion pistol to use metallic cartridges for around $5. Independent gunsmiths were doing conversions in the field as well, probably for less. Wilson notes that Colt factory records indicate a total of 46,100 cap-and-ball models were either converted to or built as cartridge revolvers, in addition to those converted in the field.

"In the 1870s, there was a growing demand for cartridge conversions," says Wilson. "Signal events in United States history were the completion of the transcontinental railroad in 1869, the post-Civil War opening of the Wild West, and the series of Indian Wars waged in the 1870s into the 1890s. The Colt revolver in the hands of sheriffs, marshals, outlaws, gunfighters, Wells Fargo agents, cowboys, ranchers, miners, sodbusters, and Indians was quickly enshrined in American folklore."

Despite the number of Colt models on the market, Remington also continued to do quite well with its own conversions for the .44 caliber Army and .36 caliber Navy models, along with pocket pistols and a handful of new small-caliber cartridge models built prior to the introduction of Remington's first all-new, large-caliber cartridge revolver introduced in 1875. From that point on, the Colt Single Action Army, 1875 Remington, and S&W Schofield were the three most highly regarded revolvers in America.

The greatest evolution of the black powder pistol occurred between 1868 and 1873, during which time the metallic cartridge conversion came to the fore as the most advanced form of personal armament. With the metallic cartridge, it was now possible to reload more quickly, and shoot with greater reliability.

The 1871-72 Open Top was the true transitional model between the Richards-Mason cartridge conversions and the 1873 Peacemaker. Around 7,000 were produced in .44 caliber rimfire. They are easily distinguished by the non-rebated cylinder, straight frame (no step down), and solid lug barrel with rear sight. (Dow and Russelle Heard Collection)

(Over Leaf)

The .46, .44, and .45 caliber Army revolvers were the most significant Remington cartridge conversions of the post-Civil War era. Pictured are six different variations. Moving clockwise from the top right, a Springfield .44 centerfire experimental, .46 caliber rimfire New Model Army, .44 caliber centerfire New Model Army, a Rollin White patent five-shot .45 rimfire (on top of holster), a nickel-plated, five-shot .44 centerfire, and a Beals .44 centerfire. (J. D. Hofer Collection)

CHAPTER 4

Remington Cartridge Conversions

From The Rollin White Patent To The 1870s

Remington was one of America's oldest arms makers, founded in 1816 by Eliphalet Remington, II. The company did not at first manufacture guns, only barrels, and did so quite successfully. In 1828 Remington moved to larger facilities in Ilion, New York, along the Erie Canal, a major trade route in the 19th century. It wasn't until 1848, following the purchase of the Ames Company of Chicopee, Massachusetts, that Remington produced an entire gun, a breech-loading percussion carbine built under contract to the U.S. Navy. It was followed by a contract for 5,000 U.S. Model 1841 percussion "Mississippi" rifles.[1] As for pistols, nearly a decade would pass before E. Remington & Sons introduced their first handgun, the Remington-Beals pocket revolver, patented June 24, 1856 and May 26, 1857. Fordyce Beals designed the gun for

Remington and shared not only the name but the patent rights as well. Beals would design many of Remington's most successful models throughout the 1860s and 1870s.

It is worthy of note that E. Remington & Sons, which was headed in later years by Eliphalet Remington's eldest son, Philo,[2] prospered well into the post-Civil War era and the American expansion West, but suffered a severe reversal of fortune in the mid-1880s and was forced into receivership in 1886. The company was reorganized two years later as the Remington Arms Company under the control of Marcellus Hartley and the New York sporting good firm of Hartley & Graham, which had played a significant role during the Civil War supplying the Union with arms and ammunition. Remington later merged with Hartley & Graham and the Union

The experimental Springfield Armory cartridge conversion on the Remington Army utilized a two-piece cylinder (similar to the type used on the smaller-caliber Remington-Rider, New Model Police and New Model Pocket revolvers) and was chambered for .44 centerfire cartridges. As shown in the close-up, the back cap had six floating firing pins and the cylinder and cap locked together with two interconnecting flanges. This is the same basic approach used today by Kenny Howell of R&D Gunshop, in the design of his Remington cartridge conversion cylinders. (J. D. Hofer Collection)

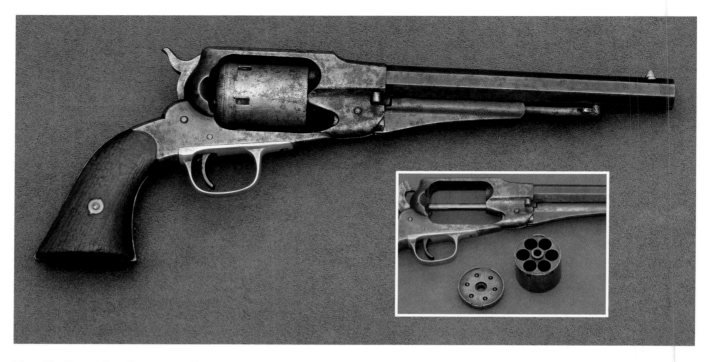

Metallic Cartridge Company (founded by Hartley after the Civil War) becoming Remington-U.M.C. in 1912. [3]

Introducing its first percussion handgun in 1857, Remington had barely gotten its feet wet in the revolver business when the Civil War broke out. Nevertheless, the advanced design of the 1861 Army Model Revolver and improved 1863 New Model Army made them one of the most popular sidearms of the Union forces during the war, second only to the Colt 1860 Army.

Always looking for a sales advantage, the New York arms maker produced one of the very first double-action revolvers in America, the Remington-Rider, named after Ohio inventor Joseph Rider who

joined the company in the late 1850s. The Rider pistols, introduced in 1860 were among the earliest to be converted to fire metallic cartridges, and the first cartridge-firing, double-action revolvers in America.

More significant, however, was the Remington New Model Army, an improvement of the original 1858 Remington-Beals Army, and the ideal large-caliber revolver for a cartridge conversion. Between 1863 and 1875 more than 120,000 percussion models were produced, many of which Remington converted to fire metallic cartridges beginning in 1868. This followed lengthy negotiations between S&W and Remington. An agreement was finally reached in February 1868 with Remington agreeing to pay a licensing fee of $1 per gun to S&W. A total of 4,574

Remington New Model Army percussion models were converted to fire the .46 caliber rimfire metallic cartridge. S&W sold the majority of the guns to Benjamin Kittredge, a wholesale and retail firearms dealer in Cincinnati, Ohio, who had initiated the request for the cartridge conversion models through S&W in 1867.

The conversions required the manufacture of a new cylinder, since six .46 caliber rounds would not fit within the diameter of the original six-shot percussion cylinder, thereby ruling out the possibility of cutting off the back and boring the chambers though. The .46 caliber Remington conversions only chambered five rounds, but they were five big ones.

Here is a Remington New Model Army, c.1868-69 early or first conversion with five-shot .46 caliber cylinder. Note the 1855 Rollin White patent date on the cylinder. This was required as part of the agreement between Remington and Smith & Wesson. (J. D. Hofer Collection)

The back of the frame, where the cylinder butted up against the recoil shield, was dovetailed to accept a new recoil plate, which was fitted between the back of the frame and the cylinder, and fastened with a small screw. The right side of the recoil shield and frame were deeply channeled to allow the loading and extracting of cartridges, however, there was no loading gate. A slot for an ejector assembly was dovetailed into the right side of the barrel lug and the ejector housing secured by a longer loading lever screw passing through the lug from the left side. The right tab of the cylinder pin was also cut off to allow

the ejector assembly to fit, and a slot was cut out of the loading lever to provide a resting place for the L-shaped tip of the ejector rod. The majority of early .46 caliber conversions, however, were not fitted with cartridge ejectors. Reshaping the front portion of the hammer into a firing pin completed the conversion.

The same basic design was used for later models chambered to the new .44 caliber Martin centerfire and Remington .45 caliber centerfire cartridges. These later designs, introduced in the summer of 1869, were six-shot revolvers and offered the cartridge ejector. The legendary Buffalo Bill Cody, a

Another rare model is the Beals Remington conversion to .44 caliber centerfire. The Beals design was the original 1858 Army percussion model of which approximately 1,900 were built. The squared shape of the loading lever and German silver cone front sight helps distinguish the Beals from later models. In 1870-71 the Ordnance Department sold approximately 15,000 surplus percussion Army revolvers, some of which were Remington-Beals models, later converted by an independent contractor to .44 centerfire. One of the distinguishing characteristics of these non-factory conversions is that the breech plate is welded to the inside surface of the recoil shield and the cylinder has been cut and a new rear section welded on. The example shown has the number 13 etched into the loading channel. The reason for this is unknown. (J. D. Hofer Collection)

The most successful of the Remington cartridge conversions was the New Model Army .44 centerfire. These later examples, c. 1870, were offered with the hand ejector. The frame was dovetailed to allow the ejector assembly to slide into place and then secured by the loading lever screw passing through from the left side of the frame. A small notch was cut into the loading lever to allow a rest for the "L" shaped tip of the ejector rod. All Remington cartridge conversions retained their percussion loading levers since it also held the cylinder pin in place when latched. Note the new "pinched" front sight, another distinguishing feature of the 1863 New Model Army. (Calvin Patrick Collection)

civilian working as an Army scout during the Indian wars (whose valor earned him the Medal of Honor in 1872) helped to make the Remington .44 one of the most famous revolvers in America, claiming that, "It never failed me."[4]

Remington's New Model Navy was the next percussion revolver to get the conversion treatment beginning in 1872-73. It was chambered for either .38 rimfire or .38 centerfire cartridges. The Navy was also the first model to come standard with both a loading gate and cartridge ejector.

Just as Colt's was doing in the early 1870s, Remington produced both new conversions while modifying older percussion models sent to the

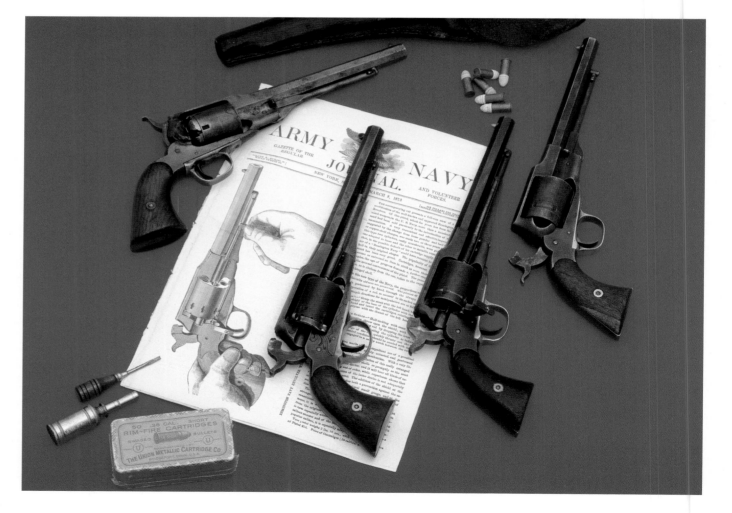

Second to the Army conversions in popularity were the early Navy and New Model Navy revolvers. Pictured at the top left is an 1868 Beals Navy with two-piece cylinder chambered for .38 rimfire; on the Remington advertisement for the .38 caliber rimfire is an engraved New Model Navy; to the immediate right an Old Model Navy c. 1870-71 converted to .38 centerfire and showing the loading gate opened; and at the far right a private armory conversion of an early Beals Navy chambered for .38 centerfire with the breech ring welded to the cylinder. Possibly done at the Whitneyville Armory, this model has no ejector and the recoil shield is not channeled, thus the cylinder would have to be removed for loading and unloading. (J. D. Hofer Collection)

The New Model Navy was the first factory conversion to feature a loading gate. The Navy breech rings were much wider than the Army conversions and extended into the original cylinder opening. The New Model Navy conversions had a channeled recoil shield, and rectangular slotted cylinder stops whereas earlier non-factory Model 1861 Navy conversions had rectangular cylinder stops, thin breech plates and no loading gate. Also note the firing and safety notches at the back of the cylinder. (J. D. Hofer Collection)

Here is a trio of Remington Navy conversions showing two-piece cylinders, an engraved New Model Navy (with loading gate and ejector), and the rare Beals conversion. (J. D. Hofer Collection)

The New Model Navy design featured a hinged loading gate with a spring latch pin that locked into the top of the breech ring.

Close-up of the early Beals Navy shows detail of the breech ring welded to the cylinder. The hammer face has been modified for centerfire cartridges. Very few examples of the Beals Navy were converted to use centerfire metallic cartridges. (J. D. Hofer Collection)

factory by the military or civilian owners. In 1875, for example, the U.S. Navy contracted to have 1,000 New Model Navy percussion revolvers used during the Civil War returned to Remington for conversion to .38 centerfire. The cost of converting the Navy models was $4.25 each, including new grips and refinishing.

Following the Civil War, Remington introduced a number of new percussion models, among them the New Model Police revolver and New Model Pocket revolver, in .36 caliber and .31 caliber, respectively. Along with the Rider, all of the new pistols were offered with factory cartridge conversions, though many were also built initially as cartridge revolvers.

The New Model Police was chambered for .38 rimfire, the New Model Pocket revolvers (designed by Fordyce Beals) for .32 rimfire. Both could be converted back to percussion pistols by changing cylinders, providing greater versatility than Colt's models, which, once converted could not be fired with a percussion cylinder.

Remington's approach to the conversion of its percussion revolvers was considerably more diverse than Colt's, which had taken only one course of action with the C. B. Richards and William Mason designs.

A Two-Part Solution to Cartridge Conversions

Remington utilized several different methods, one of which followed three influential British designs, the C. C. Tevis patent (1856), J. Adams patent (1861) and W. Tranter patent (1865), all of which made use of a split cylinder. This required cutting off the back portion of the cylinder below the percussion nipples,

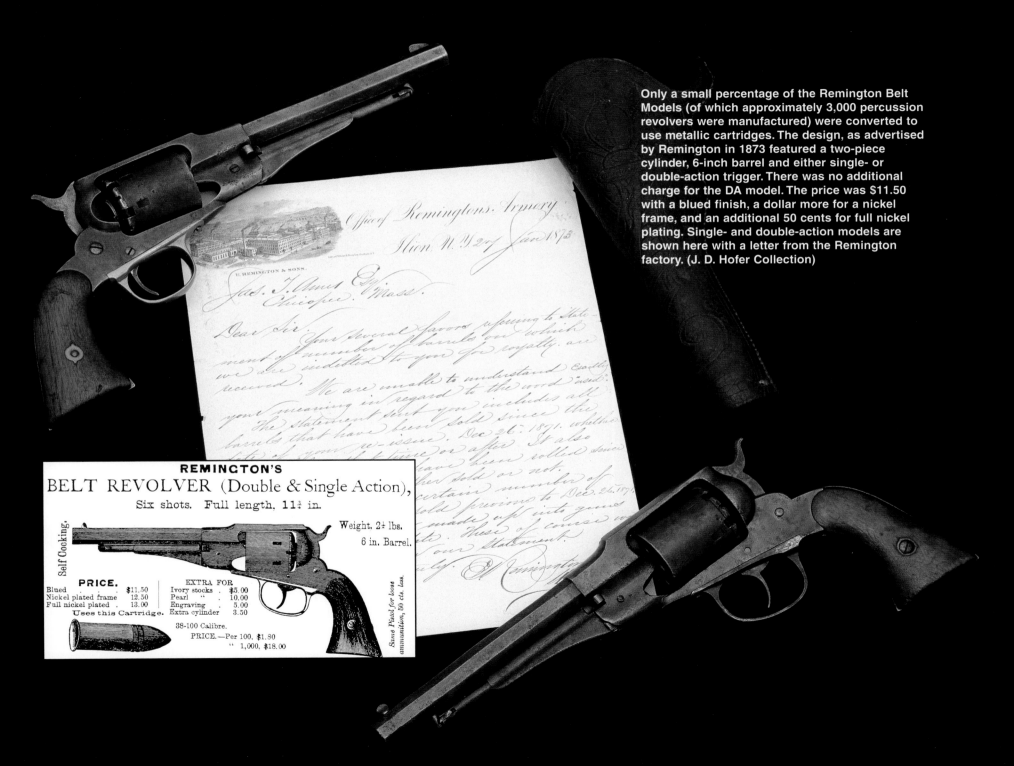

Only a small percentage of the Remington Belt Models (of which approximately 3,000 percussion revolvers were manufactured) were converted to use metallic cartridges. The design, as advertised by Remington in 1873 featured a two-piece cylinder, 6-inch barrel and either single- or double-action trigger. There was no additional charge for the DA model. The price was $11.50 with a blued finish, a dollar more for a nickel frame, and an additional 50 cents for full nickel plating. Single- and double-action models are shown here with a letter from the Remington factory. (J. D. Hofer Collection)

REMINGTON'S
BELT REVOLVER (Double & Single Action),
Six shots.   Full length, 11¾ in.

Self Cooking.

Weight, 2¼ lbs.
6 in. Barrel.

PRICE.		EXTRA FOR	
Blued	$11.50	Ivory stocks .	$5.00
Nickel plated frame .	12.50	Pearl " .	10.00
Full nickel plated .	13.00	Engraving .	5.00
		Extra cylinder .	3.50

Uses this Cartridge.

38-100 Calibre.
PRICE.—Per 100, $1.80
"   1,000, $18.00

Same Pistol for loose ammunition, 50 cts. less.

Law and order in the post-Civil War era was a tough job, and Remington offered an exemplary line of compact, five-shot, .36 caliber revolvers known as the New Model Police. Conversions to .38 caliber rimfire were produced from 1874 (a year after the percussion models were discontinued) through 1888. Pictured (clockwise from top left) are a New Model Police in .38 rimfire with 4-1/2-inch barrel; a nickel finish model with 3-1/2-inch barrel, a 6-1/2-inch model holstered, a fully engraved silver-plated model with 3-1/2-inch barrel, a William Mason conversion to .38 centerfire with 6-1/2-inch barrel, a factory converted 3-1/2-inch model with nickel finish and ivory grips in a holster, and a New Model Police with 5-1/2-inch barrel also in a holster. (J. D. Hofer Collection)

This photo shows a simple engraved .38 caliber rimfire New Model Police with 5-1/2-inch barrel, fully engraved model with 3-1/2 inch barrel, and a rare William Mason conversion in .38 centerfire. Mason was Colt's Superintendent of the Armory from 1866 to 1882, and one of the principal architects of the Richards-Mason Colt conversions. As can be seen in the picture, all New Models (except for the Mason conversion) had two-piece cylinders with safety notches between chambers on the rear of the back cap. (J. D. Hofer Collection)

This close-up shows the fitting of the two-piece cylinder. The hammer face could be rested on the slots between chambers as a safety (though not an ideal solution). The design of the hammer worked for both rimfire cartridges and the original percussion cylinder, providing the owner with two choices, metallic cartridge or loose powder.

drilling the chambers completely through and counter boring the back of the cylinder to accommodate the cartridge rims. A cylinder cap, with ratchets to engage the hand, and a pin (or pin hole) corresponding to either a pin or cutout in the cylinder (locking cap and cylinder together), completed the conversion. Fortunately, the design of the Remington hammer required only slight modification in order to work with the two-piece cylinders. Slots cut into the cap allowed the face of the percussion pistol hammer to strike the rimfire cartridges. Then by simply switching back to the percussion cylinder the gun could again be used as a conventional cap-and-ball revolver. This was fairly handy on the frontier when a box of cartridges

couldn't be found!

Approximately 18,000 New Model Police revolvers were built between 1865 and 1873, many of which were converted to fire metallic cartridge. Remington offered the Police Model with a choice of four barrel lengths: 3-1/2, 4-1/2, 5-1/2 and 6-1/2 inches with prices of $10 for the 3-1/2 and 4-1/2-inch models, $10.50 for the 5-1/2 and $11 for the 6-1/2. Options included a nickel-plated frame for an extra 75 cents, and a full nickel finish for $1.50. Ivory stocks were a whopping $5, Pearl $9, and engraving added another $5. A fancy New Model Police with 6-1/2-inch barrel would have set its owner back a total of $26.50 in 1873. A box of 100 .38 caliber rimfire cartridges cost $1.70 and a case of 1,000 rounds was $17.00.

The same conversion principle used for the New Model Police applied to the smaller, five-shot New Model Pocket Revolvers, among the most prolific of all cartridge conversions. The pocket models were manufactured as percussion revolvers from 1865 to 1873, thus there was nearly a decade of production before the conversion to .32 caliber rimfire was introduced in 1873. The pistols were available with 3-inch, 3-1/2-inch, 4-inch, and 4-1/2-inch barrel lengths, the latter two being quite rare. More than 25,000 Pocket Revolvers were produced, the majority were either converted to or produced as cartridge firing models chambered for .32 centerfire. The guns were often available with both cylinders, again making the Remington a more versatile model than a comparable Colt pocket pistol.

The five-shot Remington-Rider pocket models, also in .32 caliber, were considerably more limited with a total production between 1860 and 1873 of

Remington New Model Pocket Revolvers were offered with blued finish, nickel frame or full nickel finish. More than 25,000 were produced, with the majority converted to fire metallic cartridges with a two-piece cylinder. The one exception pictured is a C. B. Richards-type conversion to .32 caliber centerfire. This example has a channeled recoil shield similar to the early Colt cartridge conversions for the Pocket Navy. (J. D. Hofer Collection)

approximately 2,000. A good percentage of these were converted to fire metallic cartridges with a new two-piece cylinder after 1873.

While a very versatile design, the two-piece cylinder had one drawback, it had to be removed from the gun in order to be loaded or unloaded. That was less of a problem than one might think, however, as the Remington design allowed for the swift removal of the cylinder by simply dropping the loading lever, sliding the cylinder pin (base pin)

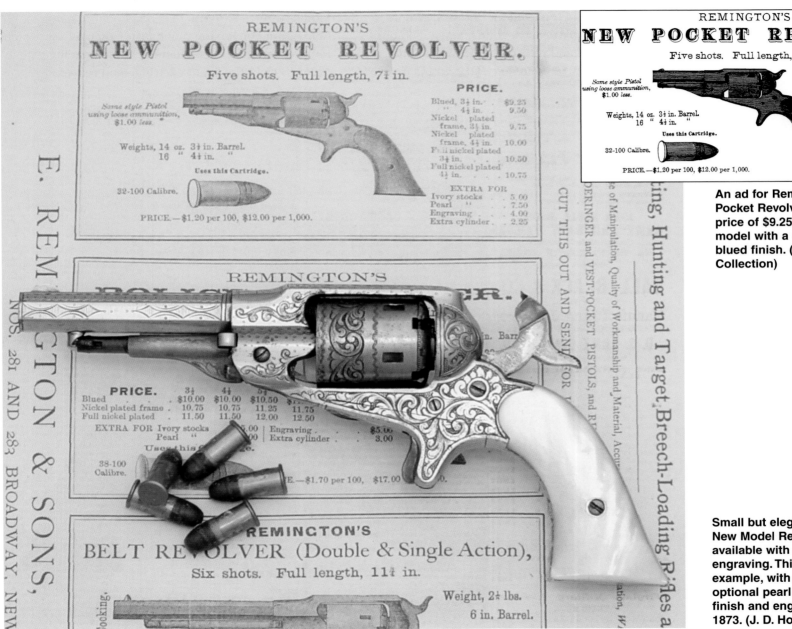

An ad for Remington's New Pocket Revolver showed a retail price of $9.25 for the standard model with a 3-1/2-inch barrel and blued finish. (J. D. Hofer Collection)

Small but elegant, the Remington New Model Revolvers were available with full factory engraving. This handsome example, with a 3-1/2-inch barrel, optional pearl grips, full nickel finish and engraving cost $22 in 1873. (J. D. Hofer Collection)

forward and rolling the cylinder out of the frame. This took only a matter of seconds, and a cylinder could be emptied and reloaded quickly (as Clint Eastwood demonstrated in *Pale Rider* with a New Model Army). With practice, one could reload a Remington conversion much faster than a Colt, which required rotating each chamber to the loading gate in order to eject the spent cartridge and reload.

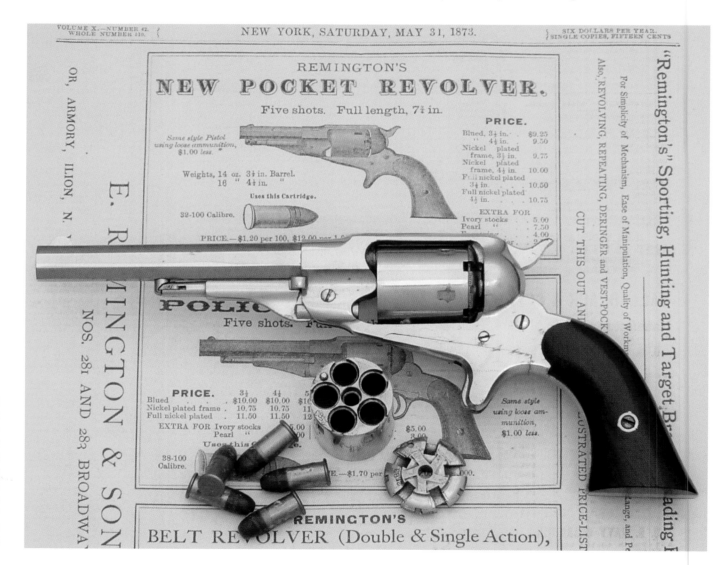

A New Model Pocket Revolver with full nickel finish and a 4-1/2-inch barrel is shown with an extra two-piece cylinder. Note the narrow hammer safety slots between the chamber slots. The small pin on the cylinder lined up with a hole in the cap to lock both halves together. The ratchet on cylinder cap engaged the hand to rotate the cylinder. (J. D. Hofer Collection)

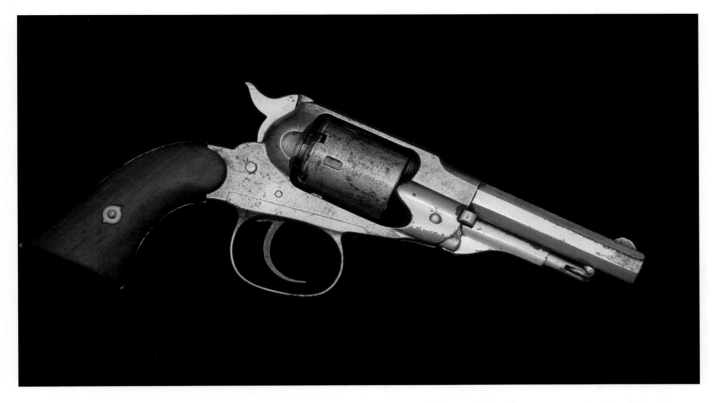

Of course, Smith & Wesson made both designs obsolete in 1870 with the introduction of the Model No. 3 Single Action top-break revolver, featuring an automatic ejector that kicked all six spent cartridge cases out of the cylinder at once as the barrel pivoted down.

Among the more rare of Remington conversions are the Belt Model revolvers, which were smaller than the New Model Army and Navy but larger than the .38 caliber New Model Police, and carried six rounds. It is estimated that no more than 3,000 Belt Models were produced and only a fraction of those

converted from .36 caliber percussion to .38 caliber rimfire. Even more rare is the Remington-Rider Double Action New Model Belt Revolver, which was identical in all other respects to the Single Action except for the trigger mechanism. Both SA and DA models utilized a six-shot, two-piece cylinder and had 6-1/2-inch octagonal barrels.

Back in 1868 Remington had taken the initiative to pursue the cartridge conversion market regardless of the White patent, which would expire less than three months after the first .46 caliber Army revolvers were introduced. Colt's was by now into production with the Thuer conversion line, which while more aesthetically pleasing was infinitely less practical than the Remington rimfire cartridge revolvers.

The Remington was also an easier revolver to convert in the field. A skilled gunsmith could copy the factory design and make the necessary parts to convert an 1858 Army or New Model Army into a cartridge revolver, including a new cylinder. And this would have been far easier after 1869 when the .44 caliber cartridge became readily available. The smaller diameter of the rounds would have permitted the existing percussion cylinder to be used for the conversion. (The diameter of the .46 caliber rimfire cartridges was such that the wall thickness of the chambers would have been too thin if a percussion cylinder were bored out for six rounds). A field conversion probably wouldn't have had an ejector assembly or channeled recoil shield, and most often either a two-piece cylinder welded together (after cutting away the portion containing the percussion nipples), or a thick back-plate welded to the inside surface of the recoil shield.[5] Similar designs, using a two-piece cylinder, are the most common contemporary cartridge conversions used today for reproduction Remington Army and Navy models.

This is another rare example of the New Model Pocket. This one utilizes a Richards-type conversion with a breech ring and channeled recoil shield for loading and unloading. The revolver is chambered for .32 caliber centerfire cartridges. (J. D. Hofer Collection)

The Remington-Rider Pocket Pistols were the smallest of the cartridge conversions. These diminutive revolvers, often dressed up with ivory grips, nickel finishes, and engraving, really were pocket-sized, as evidenced by the assortment of period accessories pictured with these four examples. At top left is a model with a 2-inch barrel that was made to fire .32 rimfire (a cartridge version without a capping channel in the recoil shield), below it is an engraved model with the 3-inch barrel, to the right is a .32 rimfire standard model, and at top right is a lightly engraved model with ivory grips. (J. D. Hofer Collection)

The .36 caliber Remington Navy was also an excellent candidate for conversion, having the same basic design as the larger .44 caliber Army. The earliest designs were on the Remington-Beales Navy models but the majority of conversions were performed on the New Model Navy revolvers c.1863-1878. The Navy models were fitted with a hinged and latched loading gate and nearly all came with an ejector assembly. The factory conversions sold for $9 and were chambered for .38 caliber rimfire cartridges. Later models (c.1874) were available in .38 caliber centerfire.

By 1875 Remington had converted or built thousands of cartridge revolvers in a variety of

This is a great pair of Remington-Rider .32 rimfire pocket pistols showing light and profuse engraving styles and ivory grips. In 1873 the model at the top right would have sold for $18. A box of 100 cartridges cost $1.20. The five-shot Remington-Rider was the first double-action cartridge revolver built in America. Remington used a two-piece cylinder for the conversion. (J. D. Hofer Collection)

calibers and models. The 1861 New Model Army conversion went out of production in 1875 with the debut of Remington's first all-new cartridge model, the 1875 Single Action Army. The .38 caliber 1863 New Model Navy conversion, however, remained in production for another three years, and conversions of the New Model Police were done as late as 1888. The Belt Model was discontinued in 1873, as were the Remington-Rider Double Action versions.

For E. Remington & Sons, the era of the cartridge conversion was nearing an end.

[1] *Flayderman's Guide to Antique American Firearms* 7th Edition.
[2] Eliphalet Remington died in 1861, at which time management of the company was taken over by his sons Philo and Samuel Remington.
[3] *Flayderman's Guide to Antique American Firearms* 7th Edition.

[4] *Buffalo Bill's Wild West—An American Legend* by R. L. Wilson. *Flayderman's Guide to Antique American Firearms* 7th Edition.
[5] *A Study of Colt Conversions and Other Percussion Revolvers*, R. Bruce McDowell.

This is an 1873 advertisement for the cartridge conversion Remington-Rider. Note that you could still buy the percussion model for a dollar less. (J. D. Hofer Collection)

71

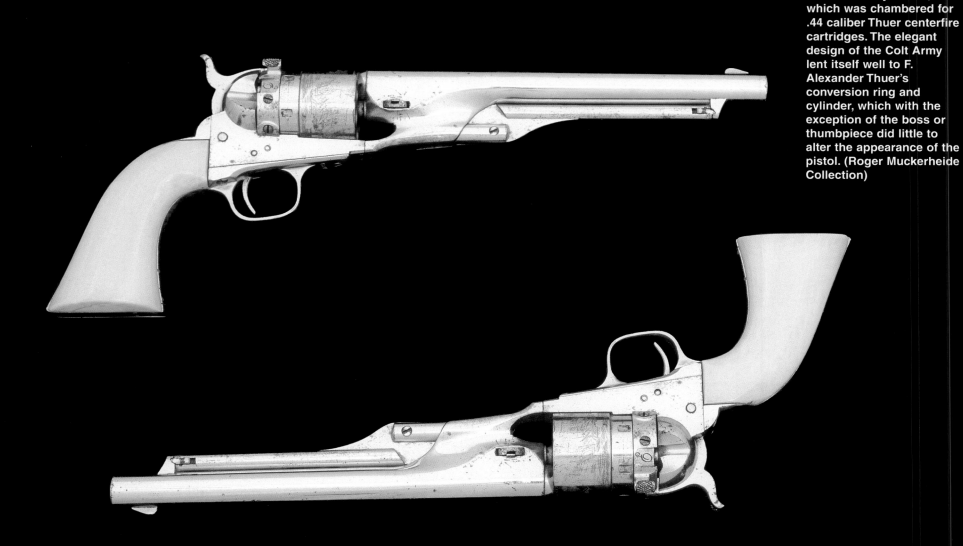

The Thuer alteration was most commonly seen on the 1860 Army model, which was chambered for .44 caliber Thuer centerfire cartridges. The elegant design of the Colt Army lent itself well to F. Alexander Thuer's conversion ring and cylinder, which with the exception of the boss or thumbpiece did little to alter the appearance of the pistol. (Roger Muckerheide Collection)

CHAPTER 5

Colt's Attempt to Circumvent the Rollin White Patent

The Thuer Conversions and Experimental Designs

olt's had missed an opportunity that, at the time, hadn't appeared to be of any great significance. When Samuel Colt dismissed Rollin White's patent for the bored-through, breech-loading cylinder design in 1855, the metallic cartridge was perceived by most American arms makers as more of a curiosity than a far-reaching innovation. A decade later the Civil War had changed that perception, but for Colt's there was nothing that could be done until the White patent, and the iron-fisted grip Smith & Wesson held on its rights, expired in April 1869.

Prior to the expiration of the White patent, Colt's had experimented with bored-through cylinders on a variety of percussion models, a Third Model Dragoon chambered for the .44 caliber Henry rimfire cartridges, a small caliber 1849 Pocket Pistol,

an 1860 Army (a design that would later influence the 1871-72 Open Top), and an 1861 Navy chambered for .38 caliber cartridges. Colt even built a Pocket model fitted with a two-piece cylinder, and a pinfire conversion utilizing a Lafaucheux design adapted to an 1851 Navy. Most were viable designs, however, none could be manufactured for sale, since there would be patent violations. The only way for Colt's to legally circumvent the White patent was to find a means of loading a metallic cartridge other than at the breech. Logically, there was only one alternative (although others would be tried) and that was to load the cartridge from the front of the cylinder. Enter F. Alexander Thuer, a Colt's employee since 1849, an inventor, and a factory marksman who spent a significant amount of time traveling the country demonstrating Colt percussion revolvers.

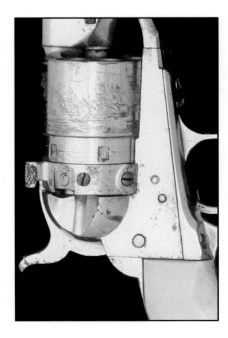

This 1860 Army Thuer conversion with British proof marks is the only known cased example to be fitted with the attachable shoulder stock. The revolver also has a unique finger rest forward of the trigger guard to help steady the pistol, while keeping one's hand out of harm's way from the cylinder blast, when fired as a carbine. (Bobby Vance Collection)

In September 1868, Thuer received patent No. 82258 for a metallic cartridge conversion system that did not infringe upon the Rollin White patent. Thuer assigned the patent to Colt's Manufacturing and production of the Thuer alteration (the term used in Colt's journals and correspondence) began late in 1869.

Somewhat generic in its legal description, the Thuer conversion was intended for a "...pistol or rifle which has a revolving chambered breech or cylinder capable of being loaded from the front, the principal object of the said invention being to produce a device by which a revolver adapted for the use of loose ammunition can at a small cost be changed, so that cartridges having primed metallic shells may be used."

In theory, the Thuer alteration was a brilliant design. In practice, it would prove to be less than ideal, but for Colt's it was the only game in town. The Hartford arms maker immediately seized on the opportunity to convert a variety of its post-Civil War percussion revolvers to the new design, despite its inherent shortcomings. Beginning in 1869 the Thuer conversion gave Colt's a cartridge-firing model to compete in a market segment that had been dominated by Smith & Wesson for a decade.

During the Civil War an estimated 129,000 Colt 1860 Army revolvers were issued, several thousand of which were modified to accept an attachable shoulder stock. There were cutouts in the recoil shield to engage the shoulder stock yoke, and a fourth screw in the frame for support. The butt strap was also notched to receive the shoulder stock screw catch. Note that on the Thuer conversion (and later percussion models above serial number 50,000) the fourth screw was not used to secure the shoulder stock. (Bobby Vance Collection)

Colt's had experimented with cartridge conversions while the White patent was still in effect. Pictured is a very rare Third Model Dragoon (in the 12300 or 12400 serial number range) converted to fire .44 Thuer centerfire. Note the fine scroll engraving with a panel scene on the barrel lug. The gun at the bottom was an experimental factory conversion No. 15703, chambered for .44 caliber rimfire. This example originally from the John R. Hegeman collection, features a specially manufactured cylinder of two-sections and a channeled recoil shield to allow loading and unloading without the need to remove the cylinder. (Photo courtesy R. L. Wilson)

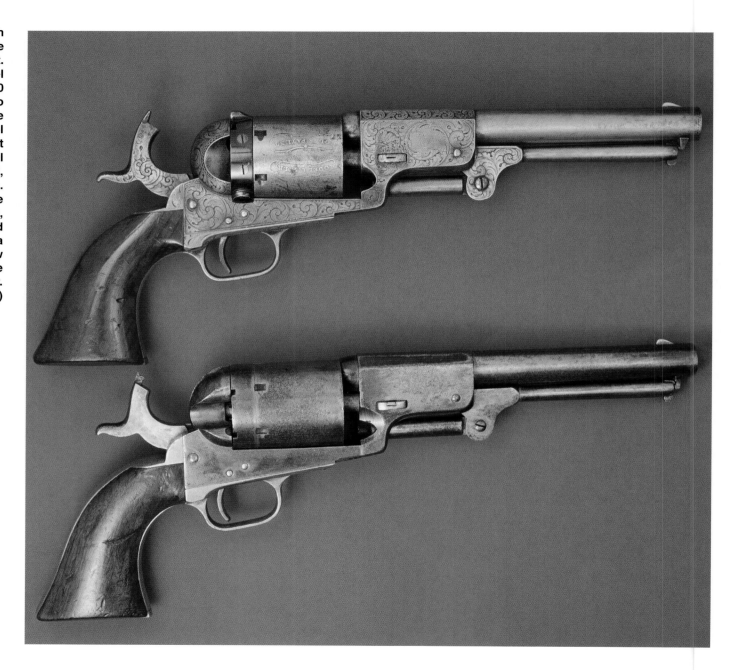

Following the licensing agreement with S&W in 1868, even Colt's oldest competitor, E. Remington & Sons had a distinct advantage over the arms maker from Hartford.

The Thuer mechanism (as shown in the patent drawings) was a rather arcane design that could be adapted to any Colt cap-and-ball revolver and was produced in sizes to fit all Colt frames. Regardless of the model, the operation was basically the same and relatively simple compared to the intricacies of loading a percussion revolver.

Colt sales literature described the loading procedure as follows: "Bring the hammer to half cock. See that the boss or projection on the ring in the rear of the cylinder is moved in position to the

An example of the evolution of Colt's conversions is evidenced by this pair: an 1851 Navy converted to the Thuer alteration and an 1862 Pocket Navy chambered for .38 rimfire, with the Richards-Mason cartridge conversion, c. 1873. The Pocket Navy version shown, has a loading gate (many did not) and no ejector. (Ex-Hable Collection. Photo courtesy R. L. Wilson)

Among the most rare of Thuer conversions are those done on the 1849 Pocket Pistol. The superb cased example with a 4-inch barrel displays all of the patented Thuer loading tools. The tapered profile of the Thuer centerfire cartridge is clearly shown by the three .31 caliber rounds sitting in the lid. Note that the cased Thuer model also came with the original percussion cylinder. (Photo courtesy R. L. Wilson)

This exquisite Thuer 1860 Army, No. 185326/I.E., is gold- and silver-plated and fitted in an elaborate rosewood case. Once again both the percussion and Thuer cylinders are included as well as a box of Thuer cartridges. (Dr. Joseph A. Murphy Collection. Photo courtesy R. L. Wilson)

right of the hammer. Hold the pistol in the left hand, muzzle upwards, thumb and forefinger grasping the cylinder, hammer to the left, butt resting on the breast. Insert the cartridges and ram them *home* in the usual manner."

It seemed to be a very practical and efficient means of loading. The self-contained black powder cartridge was far easier to handle than loose powder,

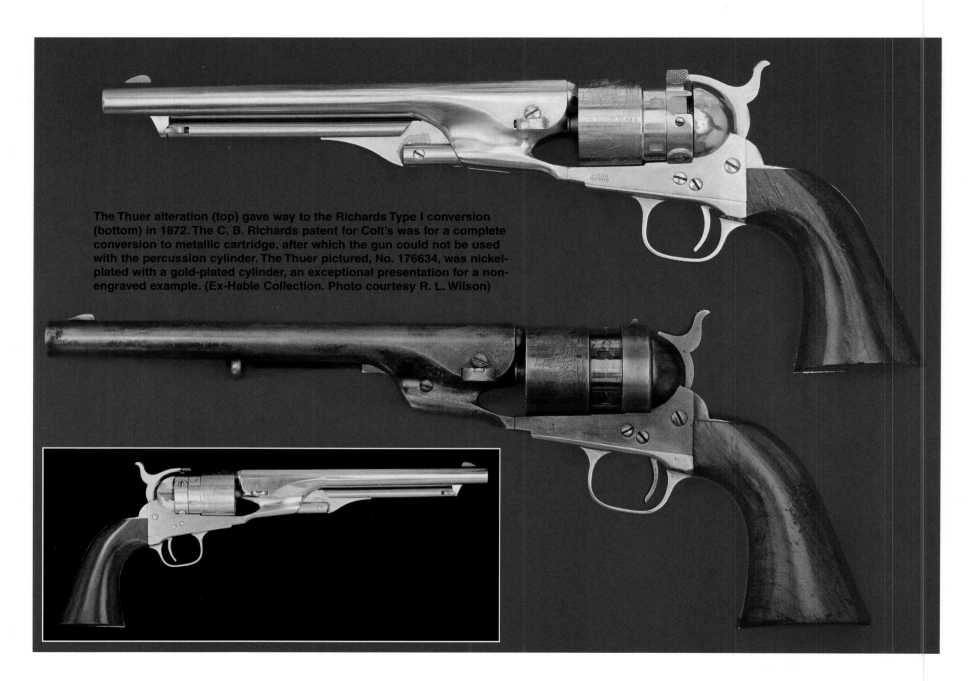

The Thuer alteration (top) gave way to the Richards Type I conversion (bottom) in 1872. The C. B. Richards patent for Colt's was for a complete conversion to metallic cartridge, after which the gun could not be used with the percussion cylinder. The Thuer pictured, No. 176634, was nickel-plated with a gold-plated cylinder, an exceptional presentation for a non-engraved example. (Ex-Hable Collection. Photo courtesy R. L. Wilson)

a ball, and a percussion cap. Ramming the cartridges into the chambers was simple. Extracting the spent shell casings was not. And here lay the problem with the Thuer conversion.

The cartridge ejection procedure as described in the instruction manual required the shooter to, "Move the boss on the ring in rear of the cylinder to the *left* of the hammer. Then cock and snap the pistol until all of the shells are ejected. Then move the boss on the ring back to the *right* of the hammer, and the pistol is ready for reloading." This process could be compared to the hand ejection of spent shells from a bored-through cylinder, and the time to accomplish either task was likely about the same. Emptying the Thuer, however, seemed a more laborious task since the gun had to be cocked and fired six more times, assuming that the cases were ejected on the first snap. The manual noted that "...should the *first* blow fail to eject the cartridge; it should be repeated."

On the plus side for the Thuer, when a box of preloaded cartridges was not available, one could use the patented Thuer cartridge loader to make bullets, reusing empty cases fitted with a fresh primer, a measure of black powder, and a cast conical lead bullet. The Thuer loading tool, patented January 4, 1870, used the cylinder pin to hold the loading dies, and the rammer to first seat a new primer in the case and then the bullet. In a worst-case scenario, the Thuer breech ring and cylinder could be easily removed and the percussion cylinder replaced. The Colt Thuer, (like the later Remington Pocket, Police and Rider models), was two guns in one and came cased with both percussion and cartridge cylinders.

The Thuer alteration was offered on the 1849

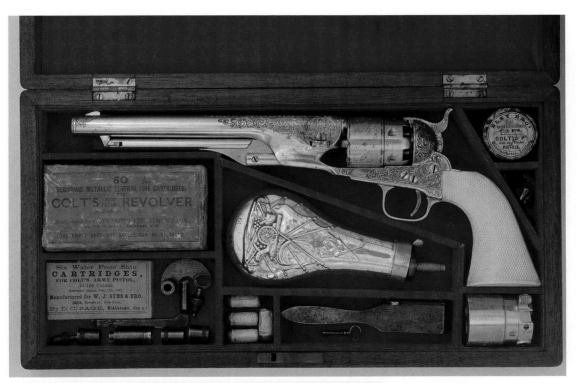

Thuer conversions were often highly embellished and this is another superb example of an 1860 Army, No. 185375/E, with elaborate scroll engraving, nickel finish and checkered ivory stocks. Once again note that the revolver is cased with both percussion and Thuer cylinders. (Ex-Hable Collection. Photo courtesy R. L. Wilson)

No Thuer, nor any Colt revolver for that matter, was more elaborate than those fitted with the beautifully cast, silver-plated Tiffany-style grips. This 1861 Navy, conversion No. 14518/E, was engraved by Louis D. Nimschke, one of the premier artisan engravers of the period. The Navy model was supplied with both percussion and Thuer loading tools. (Ex-Hable Collection. Photo courtesy R. L. Wilson)

Pocket, 1851 Navy, 1861 Navy, 1860 Army (the premier version), Pocket Pistol of Navy caliber, and the 1862 Pocket Police. Dragoon revolvers and Sidehammer pistols and rifles were also manufactured but these are considered as experimental only. [1]

The breech ring was designed to fit into place against the recoil shield, with the ratchet (machined on a collar-shaped extension from the breech of the cylinder) passing through its center to engage the

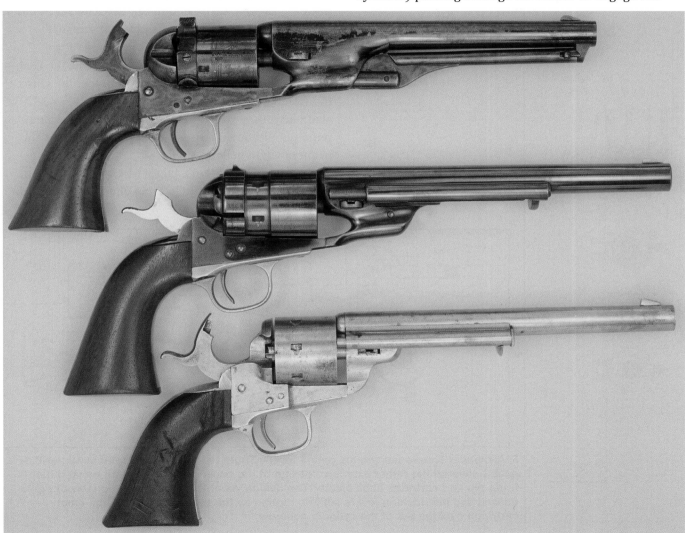

This photos shows a cartridge evolution from Colt's. Shown is (from top) a Model 1861 Navy Thuer conversion, No. 28822 (formerly Hegeman Collection), an 1860 Army Richards Type I conversion c.1872, and a prototype seven-shot Open Top Model 1871-72 Frontier. (Photo courtesy R. L. Wilson)

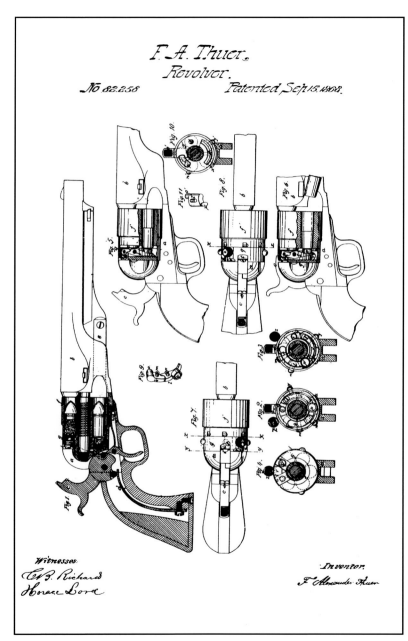

hand. As with percussion cylinders, the Thuer breech ring and cylinder combination were held in place by the center pin (arbor), barrel and wedge.

The Thuer cylinder was actually bored completely through, but since it could not be loaded from the breech, its design did not violate the White patent. The cylinder chambers had an unusual tapered bore to accommodate the shape of the cartridges, which were slightly narrower at the rear— a necessity to smooth the progress of loading with the rammer. Thuer conversion rammers (after 1870) also had a threaded opening into which a priming punch could be screwed. This was used to seat the primers when making shells.

With few exceptions, factory conversions to the Thuer alteration had the loading channel at the right

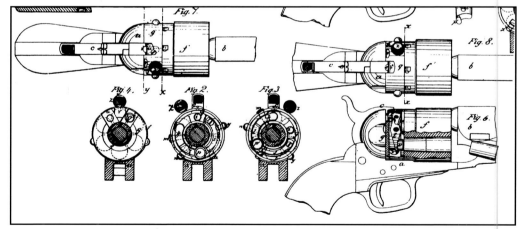

F. Alexander Thuer received his patent for the Thuer Revolver on September 15, 1868. The patent covered the rather extensive design of the conversion ring, which housed the firing pin and cartridge shell ejector. The design, as noted in the close-up view of Fig. 6., utilized two interlocking levers set into motion by the hammer to "boot" the empty cartridge casings out of the cylinder chamber.

Colt's experimented with a variety of conversion designs. This reproduction created by gunsmith R. L. Millington copies one of the earlier attempts to use a wide breech ring and one-piece cylinder chambered for .44 rimfire cartridges. The reproduction, however, is chambered for .44 centerfire.

F. Alexander Thuer c. 1868 is shown with a shoulder-stocked 1860 Army conversion. Thuer was the Colt's field representative, a marksman of some renown, who toured the country setting up exhibitions of Colt's percussion revolvers. Born in Prussia in 1826, he was 42 when he devised and patented Colt's first cartridge conversion design. Note the small pistol in Thuer's right breast pocket. (Photo courtesy R. L. Wilson)

This British proofed 1860 Army conversion is quire rare. It is the only known cased Thuer equipped with a shoulder stock. The label glued into the lid reads *Colt's Patent Fire-Arms Manufacturing Co. 17. Pall Mall, London, S.W.* and contains all of the loading, and firing instructions. (Bobby Vance Collection)

side of the barrel lug milled deeper to provide greater clearance for the loading and ejecting of cartridges. This modification, however, was rarely performed on field conversions. The lack of that machining, however, may indicate the weapon under inspection is an alteration done by a modern fabricator.

The most complicated part of the Thuer mechanism was the breech ring itself. It contained a rebounding firing pin, and an ejector mechanism, noted by the elegantly scripted "$\mathscr{E}$" to the right of the boss. The ejector consisted of two interlocking and pivoting levers, the smaller, uppermost lever, (resembling a 7 in shape) pivoted to the rear of the ring when struck by the hammer. The bottom edge engaging the top of the second lever (shaped something like an L) which then pivoted forward to "boot" the empty cartridge case out of the chamber nearest to the right of the barrel lug (Fig. 6. in the Thuer patent illustration). A third position on the ring, located between the fire and "$\mathscr{E}$" detents, provided a hammer rest as a safety. Before the gun could be discharged, the boss (or thumbpiece) had to be moved back into the firing position. It wasn't an ideal solution, but it worked.

Although similar, the breech rings on large-frame Colts differed from those on Pocket Pistols. The most obvious distinction was the absence of a hammer rest on the Pocket Pistols. In addition, a spring-loaded lever, pivoted within the conversion ring and extending outward just below the thumbpiece, was employed to hold the ring in the *fire* position. To eject spent shell casings the ring was rotated counterclockwise (against the spring tension) until the thumbpiece rested on the frame. The ring had to be held by hand while the cartridge cases were ejected otherwise it would automatically rebound to the *fire* position. On the large-frame revolvers a small stud was used to lock the ring into either the *fire* or "*E*" position. The big advantage to the Pocket Pistol design was that it couldn't inadvertently be left in the "*E*" position when loaded...a potentially fatal error!

The first Thuer models were offered for sale in the latter half of 1869 and all versions remained available until 1872, when they were succeeded by the Richards cartridge conversion. Owners of Colt percussion models could return their revolvers to the factory, and for a small fee have them converted to the Thuer system. Additionally, Thuer breech rings and cylinders were sold to Colt dealers and gunsmiths who performed field conversions. The number of guns converted in the field and those sent to Colt's for conversion is unknown, however, no more than 5,000 factory-built examples were made. These encompassed all model variations produced both in the United States and in London. [2]

The most common Thuer conversion is the .44 caliber 1860 Army (with British proof marks), followed by the .36 caliber 1851 Navy, .44 caliber 1860 Hartford Army model, Pocket Pistol of Navy Caliber, 1862 Pocket Police, 1861 Navy, and the very rare .31 caliber 1849 Pocket. The .44 caliber Third Model Dragoon, and First Dragoon are considered extremely rare. [3]

It is interesting to note that the Thuer cartridges, primarily manufactured and sold by Colt's, were centerfire, whereas early metallic cartridges for Colt conversions and 1871-72 Open Tops were rimfire. The reason for this is that Thuer cartridges were intended for reloading and centerfire was the logical choice since new primers could be easily seated in the

DIRECTIONS FOR USING
Colt's Metallic Cartridge Revolving Pistol.

TO LOAD THE PISTOL: Bring the hammer to half-cock. See that the boss or projection on the ring in rear of the cylinder is moved in position to the *right* of the hammer. Hold the Pistol in the left hand, muzzle upwards, thumb and fore-finger grasping the cylinder, hammer to the left, butt resting on the breast. Insert the cartridges and ram them *home* in the usual manner. The Pistol is fired in the ordinary way.

TO EJECT THE SHELLS: Move the boss on the ring in rear of the cylinder to the *left* of the hammer. Then cock and snap the pistol, until all of the shells are ejected. Then move the boss on the ring back to the *right* of the hammer, and the pistol is ready for reloading.

The loaded cartridges can be ejected by the same process as that described for ejecting the empty shells; should the *first* blow fail to eject the cartridge, it should be repeated.

CAUTION: Care must be taken to move the boss on the ring back to the *right* of the hammer after the ejection of the shells, so that the pistol will *always* be ready for firing except when the ejector is to be used.

There is a safety notch under the boss on the ring in rear of the cylinder, in which the hammer may rest when the pistol is not in use. The ring however, must be moved to the *right* in that case, so as to bring the firing-pin under the hammer, before the pistol can be fired.

The shells can be reloaded and used as often as may be required.

Office of Colt's Pat. Fire Arms Mfg. Co.
    Hartford, Conn., 1868.

Colt's made it sound quite simple to load and unload a Thuer conversion. When everything worked as advertised it was. But sometimes the cartridges wouldn't seat easily with the rammer, they wouldn't eject the first time the hammer-activated ejector was fired, and the breech ring had a tendency to bind up when fouled by black powder residue. The problems were like many experienced with cap-and-ball revolvers. The Thuer was better, but not as good as a cartridge gun with a bored-through, breech-loading cylinder.

The Thuer conversion ring and cylinder were held in place by the cylinder pin, barrel and wedge. The design allowed the revolver to be reverted back to percussion use by removing the ring and cylinder and replacing the cap-and-ball cylinder. (Bobby Vance Collection)

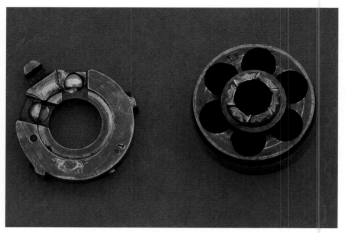

In this view, the ratchet and collar extension from the breech of the cylinder are shown. The collar, which fit within the recess of the breech ring, also prevented the cylinder from being loaded at the rear. This clearly illustrated that the Thuer alteration in no way infringed upon the White patent for the bored-through, breech-loading cylinder.

The 1860 Army was a considerably accurate weapon when fitted with the attachable shoulder stock. This London model had a finger rest added (threaded into the frame just forward of the trigger guard) to provide a better two-handed grip. (Bobby Vance Collection)

This view shows the Thuer conversion ring as it faced the recoil shield. The cylinder ratchet extended through the center of the ring to engage the hand and advance each round as the hammer was cocked. Note the British proof mark on the cylinder. The rings and cylinders were both numbered. This example is marked 01.

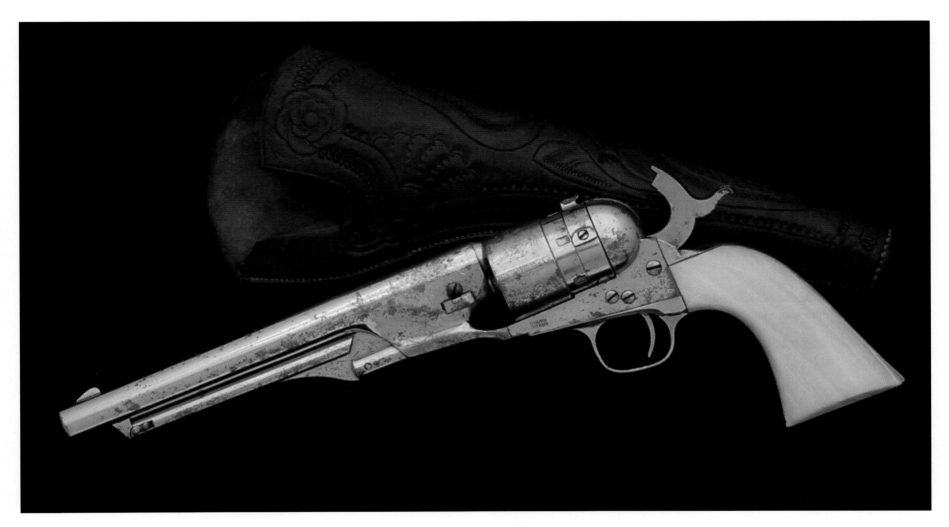

reclaimed brass shells. Thuer cartridge boxes stated: *The Empty Cartridge Shells can be Reloaded.* Another benefit of the Thuer design was that all models, including Pocket Pistols, fired six rounds, thus the smaller Pocket revolvers gained an extra shot when fitted with a Thuer conversion—an advantage even

the later Richards and Richards-Mason models did not offer. [4]

Despite the advanced design, the Thuer was not a successful gun. As R. L. Wilson noted in *The Book of Colt Firearms*, "Several points had been against the Thuer becoming a popular product in the Colt line:

Here is an 1860 Army c.1870 fitted with the Thuer alteration. The finish is nickel with ivory grips. The carved California-style holster is from the same period. (Roger Muckerheide Collection holster, George Jackson)

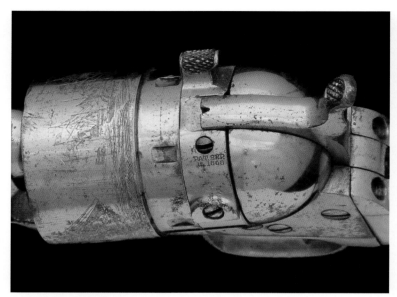

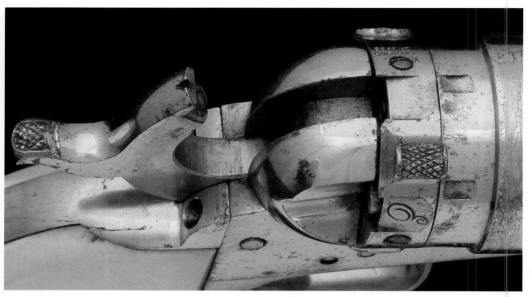

The Thuer patent date was stamped on every conversion ring.

This is the Thuer conversion ring in the firing position.

It has now been moved to the eject position.

The tapered cartridge, the special loading tools, and the easily fouled conversion ring all contributed to the poor sales showing." Interestingly, the majority of Thuer alterations known to collectors are in very good condition—"proof," wrote Wilson, "that most were seldom used."[5]

Although their rarity makes them highly desirable today among Colt collectors, the Thuer ultimately proved nothing more than a short-lived stopgap measure, or as the old black powder saying goes—a flash in the pan.

[1] The Book of Colt Firearms
[2] Ibid
[3] The Book of Colt Firearms and A Study of Colt Conversions and Other Percussion Revolvers.
[4] Historian and author R. Bruce McDowell notes that both five- and six-shot Thuer cylinders were produced for the Pocket models.
[5] R. L. Wilson notes that surplus Thuer conversion rings and unnumbered cylinders were sold in the 1920s and 1930s, and a few Colt 1860 Army revolvers were subsequently "converted" during the 20th century. These guns do not have the same collector's value as an original gun built by Colt's between 1869 and 1872. Caveat emptor.

The business side of the Thuer ring shows the firing pin (one o'clock position), and the ejector mechanism (seven o'clock position). The lip at the bottom of the lever would be driven forward by the impact of the hammer to kick the spent casings out of the chamber. At least that was the idea! The face of the hammer was fitted with a circular metal insert to prevent damage to the hammer by accidental striking against the ring when not in the proper position and the repeated striking on the ejector head.

The Richards Type I was the first breech-loading cartridge conversion model offered by Colt's. This is a rare U.S. model Richards with Springfield Armory proofs. Note that the U.S. model has a flat ejector rod tip. This example is pictured with a c. 1872 civilian single loop holster and a belt converted from a Civil War carbine sling. Also shown is an original box of .44 centerfire Martin cartridges manufactured at Frankford Arsenal, Penn. (Dow and Russelle Heard Collection)

CHAPTER 6

The C. B. Richards 1860 Army Conversions

Practical Ways to Make Old Guns New

If you look closely at the Thuer patent drawing you will see two names at the lower left, the witnesses, Horace Lord and C. B. Richards.

It was Charles B. Richards, a prominent inventor and Colt's Assistant Factory Superintendent, who really put the lead into Hartford's legendary percussion models. In 1871 he was granted patent No. 117461 for *Improvements in Revolvers*.

As described by Richards in the patent text, "My invention relates to that kind of revolver which has a chambered breech or cylinder. It has for its object to provide a compact and cheap form of this kind of arm, which shall be fitted for the convenient use of a flanged metallic cartridge, and it is particularly useful as furnishing a means of converting a revolver constructed and intended for loose ammunition into one adapted for the kind of metallic cartridges which

are loaded into the chambers from the rear."[1] The C. B. Richards patent was assigned to Colt's and intended for the alteration of the 1860 Army to .44 caliber centerfire cartridges, a process that began commercially in 1872, a year after the introduction of the new Colt .44 rimfire Open Top model. Richards and William Mason also designed the Open Top. Colt's most prominent inventor, C. B. Richards designed the 1871 Cloverleaf revolver as well, marking his third significant patent for Colt's.

The original Richards conversion, commonly referred to as the Type I or First Model, utilized a breechplate with a rebounding firing pin. The breechplate was combined with a newly manufactured cylinder, or a cap-and-ball cylinder, the percussion portion of which had been cut away, the chambers bored completely through and a new

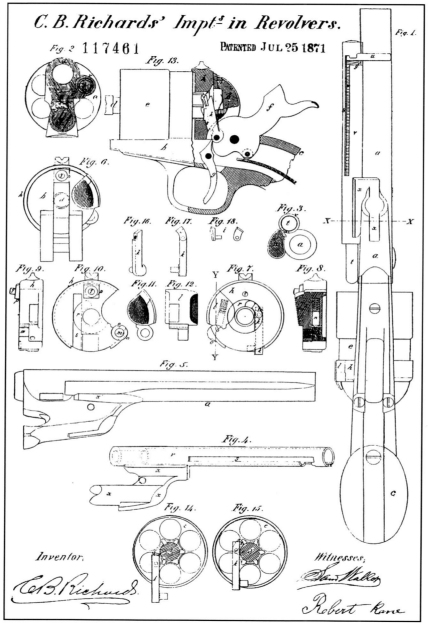

C.B. Richards' Impt? in Revolvers.

Fig. 2 117461

PATENTED JUL 25 1871

ratchet cut to engage the hand [2]. The conversion also required removing 3/16th of an inch from the face of the recoil shield into which the breechplate (also referred to as the conversion ring) was seated and secured by the cylinder pin. The breechplate measured 0.49 inches in thickness by 1.675 inches in diameter with a channel slightly larger than the size of the cylinder bore cut out of the right side to facilitate the loading and ejection of cartridges from the breech end of the cylinder. On all Richards conversions this channel was protected by a hinged loading gate attached to the breech ring. The right side of the recoil shield was also channeled for cartridge loading, however on some experimental models, and on later Richards-Mason Pocket conversions the loading gate was frequently omitted, leaving the rear of the cylinder chamber exposed.

The final alteration to the 1860 Army required the hammer face to be ground flat in order to strike the floating firing pin. The sum of these modifications were irreversible and thus ruled out the refitting of the gun with a percussion cylinder. This was a disadvantage upon which Remington capitalized in the early 1870s with their popular two-piece cylinders. A simple switch back to the percussion cylinder allowed the use of loose powder, caps, and balls in the same gun.

One of the most complicated and costly components of the Richards conversion was the cartridge ejector assembly. The newly fabricated housing (containing the ejector rod, spring, and ejector head) was attached to a metal plug that fit into the channel previously used for the loading rammer. The lug and right side of the barrel just above the rammer channel were notched to accommodate the ejector housing, which was secured by the loading lever screw passing through the lug from the left side.

Distinguishing characteristics of the Richards Type I conversion ring are the integral rear "V" sight cast into the top of the breechplate, the internal firing pin, and a 1/32nd of an inch overlap of the cylinder at the breech. When viewed from the side, the Type I breechplate shrouds the back of the cylinder, whereas on later Richards-Mason conversions there is clear separation between the face of the conversion ring and the cylinder breech.

Priced at $15, the Richards 1860 Army was produced c. 1871 to c. 1878 and it is estimated that Colt's manufactured 9,000 examples in the serial number range #1 to #8700 (excluding Richards-Mason arms from approximately #5800 through #7900).

The alteration from 1860 Army (top) to the First Model Richards was extensive. The percussion model is a four-screw example with the recoil shield cut to accept the attachable shoulder stock yoke. With the conversion ring and loading gate, it becomes obvious at a glance why shoulder stocks could no longer be used with the Richards conversions. (Dennis Russell Collection)

This pair of First Model Richards revolvers shows some subtle differences between those produced by Colt's as cartridge guns with new cylinders, and Civil War-era percussion revolvers converted to the Richards system. Note the ejector rod on the percussion conversion, which extends past the wedge slot. The percussion model also has the less commonly seen iron trigger guard. Both, however, are fitted with the second type loading gate, which has an external gate spring, indicated by the screw at the base of the breech ring beneath loading gate hinge. (Dennis Russell Collection)

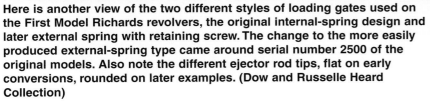

Here is another view of the two different styles of loading gates used on the First Model Richards revolvers, the original internal-spring design and later external spring with retaining screw. The change to the more easily produced external-spring type came around serial number 2500 of the original models. Also note the different ejector rod tips, flat on early conversions, rounded on later examples. (Dow and Russelle Heard Collection)

A disassembled First Model Richards displays the individual components of the C.B. Richards patent, the ejector housing, converted cylinder, modified barrel and lug, and breech ring with integral rear sight. The notches in the side of the barrel and lug were necessary to fit the ejector housing. The plug (extending from below the ejector housing) was designed to fit within the rammer channel and utilize the loading lever screw (the hole is above the rammer plug) for mounting. (Roger Muckerheide Collection)

Richards numbers are also in the percussion series, from as early as serial #167,000 to #200614. [3]

In addition to factory production models (those originally built as cartridge revolvers) and factory conversions, many 1860 Army revolvers were converted to the Richards style on the frontier. A skilled gunsmith could copy the design.

Among the rarest examples of the Richards 1860 Army conversion are those with 12 cylinder stops (rather than six), the additional set having been intended to serve as a safety, by locking the cylinder between chambers. Although the design worked, one

had to make certain that the cylinder was firmly set on the stop, otherwise it could easily rotate back to a loaded chamber. The 12-stop safety system proved more or less as effective as the slots cut between chambers on Remington percussion cylinders, which functioned similarly. The principal difficulty with the 12-stop design (as with the six-stop conversion cylinders) was that the bolt slots occasionally broke through when the percussion chambers were enlarged to accommodate .44 centerfire rounds. They also had a tendency to wear through over time and many surviving examples have one or more broken

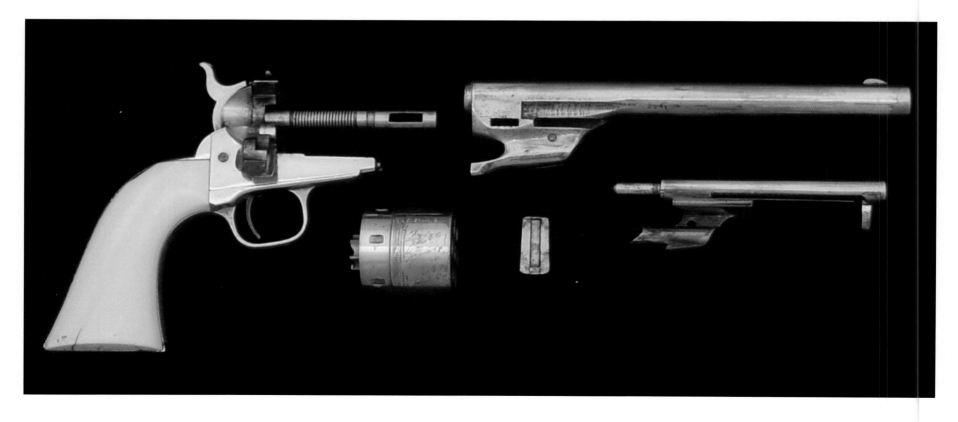

bolt slots. Ironically, the cylinder locking notches on the 12-stop rarely broke through because they were cut between the chambers.

Author Bruce McDowell's theory on the failure of the 12-stop cylinder design is perhaps the most likely. He pointed out that the 12-stop cylinder could, if not properly set or with wear to the fingers of the lock bolt, cause the action to jam. A gun that could possibly jam because of the cylinder design was a liability few could afford in the Old West.

The U.S. Richards

In 1871 the U.S. Ordnance Department ordered the conversion of approximately 1,200 U.S.-issue Model 1860 Army percussion revolvers to the Richards design for the .44 centerfire metallic cartridge. Colt's handled the alterations in Hartford, and it is believed that some of the U. S. models were also fitted with the 12-stop cylinder.

Every gun within the Ordnance Department order was stamped with a new conversion serial number located beneath the original factory stamping. This usually consisted of a two- or three-digit number with an A suffix. The new numbers were stamped on the barrel lug, cylinder, breech ring, loading gate and ejector rod arm. The military conversions were also stamped with U.S. either forward of, or just above the wedge on the left side of the barrel. On later

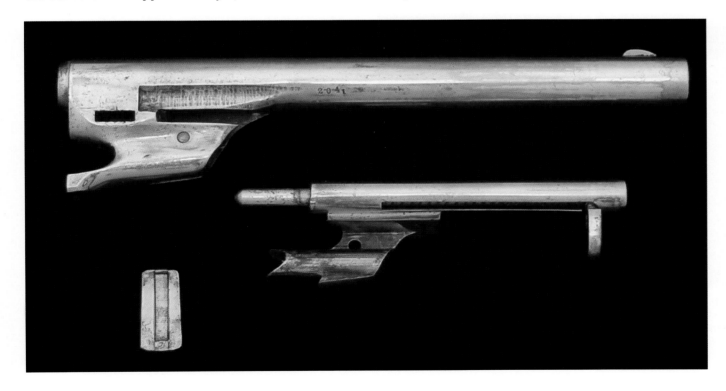

Close-up detail shows the plug for the ejector housing in relation to the rammer channel used to support the assembly. (Roger Muckerheide Collection)

This is a rare First Model Richards with the 12-stop cylinder. Note the long ejector rod and chamber bolt slots broken through. This was most common on models with converted percussion cylinders. The gun is shown with an unmarked "Slim Jim" holster and a period Buffalo Skinning knife set with checkered ivory handles. (Guns, Roger Muckerheide Collection, knife set, George Jackson Collection)

conversions the A suffix was eliminated, only the loading gate and breechplate were numbered, and the conversion number was stamped either above or below the original serial number. Springfield Armory inspector marks "A" (for O. W. Ainsworth) were present on all military conversions, and both three- and four-screw (the latter variation designed for a shoulder stock) Army models were modified. The breechplate and loading gate altered the contour of the recoil shield, narrowing the slots originally used to anchor the shoulder stock yoke. Thus the shoulder stocks could not attach to the Richards conversions as originally designed.

The U.S. Richards models were issued to and used by the Cavalry well into the 1880s, by which time the Colt Single Action Army and various S&W models made them obsolete. Good examples of the U.S. models are hard to find because of the wear and tear they experienced in military service. Civilian Richards models, however, are relatively common. The civilian models bore new serial number as well but without the A suffix, U.S. stamp or government inspector's mark seen on the military versions. The majority of civilian First Model Richards conversions had six-stop cylinders, as did most engraved specimens and *all* nickel-plated conversions. There are no known examples of an original nickel-plated Richards Army conversion with 12 cylinder notches. It is interesting to note that both the Union Metallic Cartridge Company and U.S. Cartridge Co. used a 12-stop Richards conversion to illustrate the labels on their boxes.

These Type I Richards conversions are broken down into four primary categories: the first production done in 1871 to convert military percussion revolvers to metallic cartridge; those converted at the Hartford factory using leftover percussion inventory; models built at Hartford with newly manufactured cylinders, and the 12-stop variation, both in civilian and U.S. models, of which approximately 100 were produced. It reamins questionable whether any 12-stop U.S.-marked models were originally built, though some examples exist today.

The Second Model Richards Conversion

The Richards Type I proved an expensive undertaking for Colt's because of the complexity of the breechplate design, internal rebounding firing pin, and the number of steps necessary to modify the barrel, and assemble and mount the new ejector housing.

In comparison to the simple Remington New Model Army conversions, the Richards Type I was a far more dashing and innovative design worthy of the Colt name, but it was also becoming clear to Colt's management that a less costly approach was necessary in the difficult post-Civil War environment. In 1872, William Mason, Colt's Superintendent of the Armory from 1866 to 1882, introduced a new design that simplified the conversion. Mason's *Improvements in Revolving Fire-Arms* was patented on July 2, 1872. In the interim, however, C. B. Richards introduced a second version of his design utilizing the new Mason breechplate and a firing pin riveted to the hammer. Often referred to as the Transition Richards, this second variation, produced c.1872 reduced production costs, though it still retained the

cartridge ejector assembly of the Type I. The short-lived Type II depleted remaining inventory while Colt's prepared to introduce the all-new Richards-Mason line, which would be expanded to include the 1851 Navy, 1861 Navy, and Pocket Pistols beginning in 1872-73.

This close-up shows an early First Model conversion loading gate (conversion No. 52) and a 12-stop cylinder. The rebated cylinder bolt slots often broke through because of the thinner chamber walls created by the conversion to .44 cartridges. The safety slots rarely broke through because they were cut between chambers. (Roger Muckerheide Collection)

This shows an early Type I Richards with a 12-stop cylinder (reproduction) and a factory six-stop Type I. The later six-stop models with round ejector rod tip were produced by Colt's as original cartridge guns and were fitted with new cylinders. The occurrence of broken bolt slots on new cylinders was rare. (Author's Collection and Dow Heard Collection)

It is interesting to note that while Richards models with the 12-stop cylinder were not popular, the United States Cartridge Co. of Lowell, Massachusetts, chose to picture a 12-stop model on their cartridge boxes. (Dow Heard Collection)

Conversion numbers were stamped on the ejector housing and barrel lug. This close-up also shows the fit of the ejector housing plug within the rammer channel, and the machining to the barrel lug to accommodate the base of the ejector housing. (Dow and Russelle Heard Collection)

The First Model Richards breechplate was a multifaceted contraption. In addition to having an integral rear sight (necessary because the notched sight on the percussion hammer was ground off in the conversion) it also shrouded the back of the cylinder, housed the rebounding firing pin, the loading gate, and a small metal flange protruding into the hammer rest cutout, locking the ring to the frame. It was a very well engineered device. But it was also costly to manufacture.

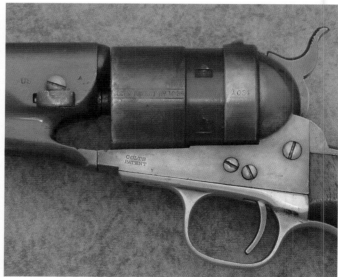

This rare U.S. Richards conversion is in relatively good condition. Note the U.S. stamp just forward of the wedge screw and "A" proof mark (to the right of the screw) indicating Springfield Armory. The conversion number, 1034, is stamped on the right side of the breech ring. (Dow Heard and Russelle Collection)

The First Model Richards design (left) gave way to the Type II (center) early in 1872. Combining the Mason cylinder and conversion ring design, the interim model saw the return of the hammer-notch rear sight, a firing pin riveted to the percussion hammer, and a simpler breech ring and loading gate. This design was carried into the Richards-Mason conversion (right) in 1872-73. (Roger Muckerheide Collection)

(Previous Page)

The swift evolution of the Colt cartridge conversion era can be seen in three models, (from top to bottom) the First and Second Richards and Richards-Mason conversions. The Richards-Mason conversions were generally not conversions at all but built as cartridge guns with a new barrel and cylinder. The new barrels (which were produced immediately after Colt's depleted its inventory of percussion barrels) are often referred to as solid-lug barrels, since they did not have the rammer cavity used for seating lead balls in percussion cylinders. The Richards-Mason models also introduced the patented William Mason ejector, designed to mount on the new solid-lug barrels. (Roger Muckerheide Collection)

The dates for both the Richards and the Mason patents, July 25, 1871 and July 2, 1872, appeared on the left side of the frame on all Transition Richards conversions. Only produced for a short time, they are among the rarest of Colt cartridge conversions.

The majority of Richards Type I and Type II conversions were done at the Hartford factory, a handful of Type I conversions were built at the Springfield Armory, while independent gunsmiths converted several hundred or more percussion models to .44 centerfire cartridges.

In the early 1870s, as the settling of the Western Frontier commenced, 1860 Army conversions to the metallic cartridge became a booming business both for Colt's and gunsmiths in every town and territory from the Mexican border to the Dakotas.

[1] *A Study Of Colt Conversions and Other Percussion Revolvers* by R. Bruce McDowell
[2] On Richards conversion cylinders the cylinder ratchet teeth were positioned between each chamber, whereas on percussion cylinders the ratchets had been in line with the chambers or nipples.
[3] *The Book of Colt Firearms* by R. L. Wilson

Nickel-plated and engraved examples of the First Model Richards are rare, and all known examples were fitted with the standard six-stop cylinder. This exquisite specimen has light cylinder and barrel engraving, and carved eagle and snake ivory grips. It is pictured with a border-stamped "California" pattern holster constructed of bridle weight leather, and a spear point Bowie knife. (Roger Muckerheide Collection. Bowie knife courtesy George Jackson)

These four exceptional versions of early Colt cartridge conversions include (from top to bottom) a rare U.S. Richards model, a Richards Type I showing the flat hammer face, Richards Type II with the Mason conversion ring and cylinder (note that both Richards and Mason patent dates are marked on the frame), and a new model Richards-Mason 1860 Army with solid-lug barrel, firing pin on the hammer and dovetailed front sight. All 1860 Army conversions came with 8-inch barrels, although some modifications to shorter lengths were certainly done after the fact. (Dow and Russelle Heard Collection)

Holsters for the civilian 1860 Richards cartridge models varied from military style, such as the hand-tooled flap holster, to the popular California pattern holsters which were the most common type in the 1860s and '70s. Wild Bill Hickok carried his 1851 Navy revolvers in similarly styled California pattern holsters. (Dow and Russelle Heard Collection)

The evolution of the Richards to Richards-Mason design is shown in this group of early 1872-73 models. Clockwise from the top is an 1861 Navy Richards-Mason conversion, an 1851 Navy in a hand-tooled California pattern holster with a sewn-in toe plug, an 1851 Navy U.S.-marked factory percussion conversion atop a California pattern holster for either left-hand draw or Hickok-style reverse right-hand draw, a nickel-plated Richards 1860 Army with ivory stocks atop another open-top style California pattern holster, an 1851 Navy in another beautifully hand-tooled open-top style California pattern holster, and an 1851 Navy in an English half-flap holster. (Dow and Russelle Heard Collection)

CHAPTER 7

Richards-Mason Conversions

Improvements and New Models

Simplicity is defined as "the state, quality, or an instance of being simple." This is a fairly broad interpretation that suits a variety of objects and individuals. It is the second definition, however, that exemplifies William Mason's 1872 patent for *Improvements in Revolving Fire-Arms*, "Freedom from complexity."

Mason took a more pragmatic approach than C. B. Richards to his design and between the two extremes evolved the Richards-Mason conversion. It was first seen in 1872.

It is interesting to note that Charles B. Richards' 1871 patent for *Improvements in Revolvers* was based on the 1860 Army, whereas Mason chose one of Colt's oldest models, the 1851 Navy. A simple gun evolved from the earliest Dragoons, the 1851 Navy was the most prolific and popular revolver then in existence. Produced for more than 20 years, 1851 through 1873, the Navy was the most successful model in Colt's

history up to that time. It was the gun favored by both lawmen and the lawless, and the pistol of choice of the legendary James Butler "Wild Bill" Hickok.

Mason's design, however, was not based solely on the conversion of 1851 Navy percussion revolvers. As the patent drawings indicate the design involves production utilizing newly manufactured components for the barrel, cylinder, and breechplate. What was to become the Richards-Mason conversion was a combination of three U.S. Patents, No. 11746 (July 25, 1871, by C.B. Richards), No. 119048 (September 19, 1871, by C. B. Richards), and No. 128644 (July 2, 1872 by William Mason, assigned to Colt's). Specifications of the latter called for "an efficient means of rotating the breech; also, for the application to the pistol of a conveniently-arranged shell ejector." This was to be the principal feature of percussion conversions and newly manufactured cartridge models utilizing percussion parts. While that may sound the same,

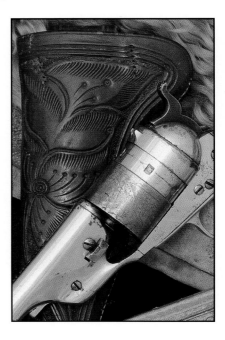

William Mason's 1872 patent was for an improvement to the Richards conversion, introducing a new ejector housing and production (or conversion) barrel design to facilitate a less costly and more efficient means of converting percussion Colts to metallic cartridges. The Mason ejector became standard on all Colt models.

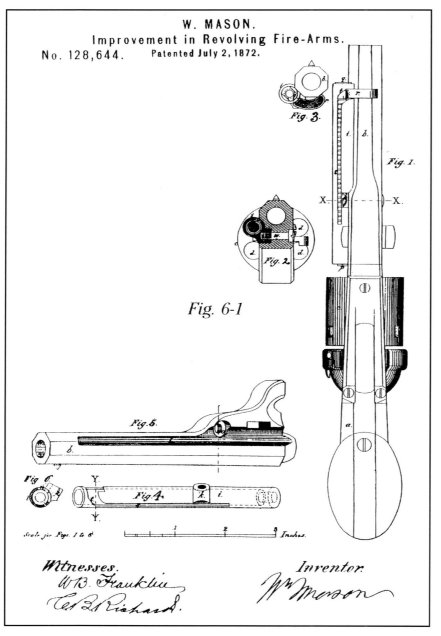

W. MASON.
Improvement in Revolving Fire-Arms.
No. 128,644.   Patented July 2, 1872.

Fig. 3.

Fig. 1.

Fig. 2.

Fig. 6-1

Fig. 5.

Fig. 6

Fig. 4.

Scale for Figs. 1 to 6   Inches.

Witnesses.
WB. Franklin
C. L. Richard.

Inventor.
Wm Mason

the applications were entirely different.

Factory production of the Richards-Mason cartridge models encompassed Colt's entire range of percussion revolvers, but just as with the Richards conversions it began with the 1860 Army, this time utilizing remaining inventory (frames and internal parts), combined with new production barrels, cylinders, and the Mason breech ring and cartridge ejector.

The key to Colt's reduction in assembly costs for the Richards-Mason conversion was the new S-lug barrel design, manufactured with a channel for the ejector housing, and a recess (forward of the wedge opening) into which a threaded stud on the Mason ejector housing was inserted and fastened to the lug by a screw passing from the right side of barrel.

The second cost-cutting measure was the Richards-Mason breech ring, which was cut away at the top, providing either a tapering hole through which a hammer-mounted firing pin could pass for centerfire models, or an off-center notch on the left, allowing the rimfire hammer to strike the cartridges. This new design eliminated the earlier Richards Type I rebounding firing pin and integral breech-ring rear sight, thus allowing the use of original percussion-style hammers with the "V- notched" hammer sight. Firing pins were mounted through either a vertical slot for centerfire, or a notch on the left of the hammer face for rimfire, and secured by two small rivets.

All 1860 Army conversions were chambered for .44 caliber centerfire cartridges. This was an interesting choice considering that the new 1871-72 Open Top, which *preceded* the Richards-Mason Army into production, was based on an 1860 Army-style frame, (without the rebated cylinder step cut) and was chambered exclusively for .44 caliber Henry rimfire cartridges. Thus in 1872 Colt's had two entirely different large-caliber cartridge models in production.

The most popular Colt conversion was also the most popular percussion model, the 1851. Shown are three examples of 1851 Navy conversions. At the top is an original cartridge model chambered for .38 caliber rimfire. This example has the solid-lug barrel and internal-spring loading gate. It is resting against an elaborately embossed flap holster produced in the 1850s. Center is a Navy percussion conversion to .38 centerfire, and at the bottom is a handsome nickel-plated Navy with scooped barrel lug. Models with the scooped lug were made from percussion inventory that had not been completed, thus only the lug was finished and not the loading lever and plunger channels. This example is chambered for .38 Long Colt rimfire. These same cartridges were also used in rifles, thereby giving their owners one bullet for both pistol and carbine. (Dow and Russelle Heard Collection)

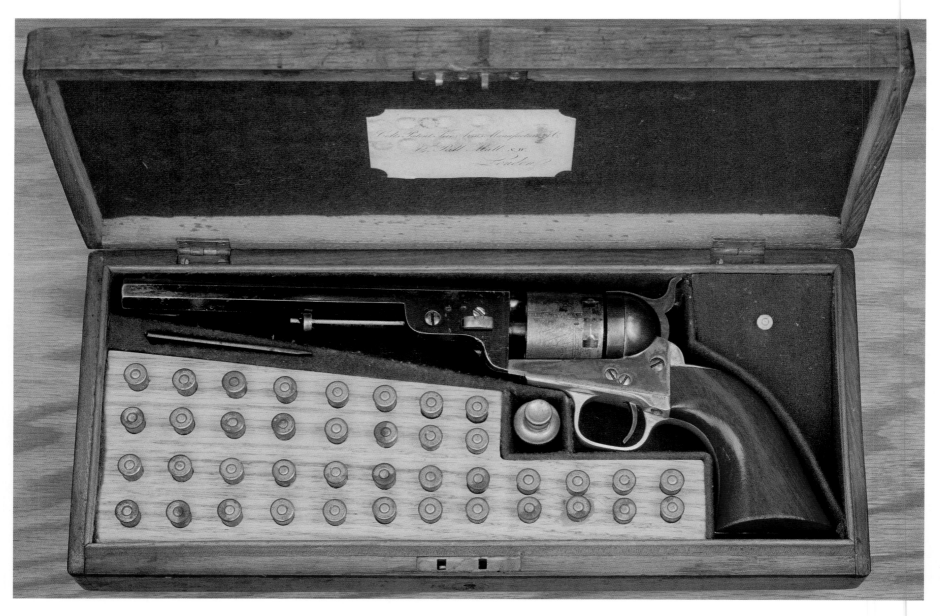

This 1851 Navy is displayed in an English oak box. Cased examples are uncommon. (Ex John B. Solley Collection. Photo courtesy R. L. Wilson)

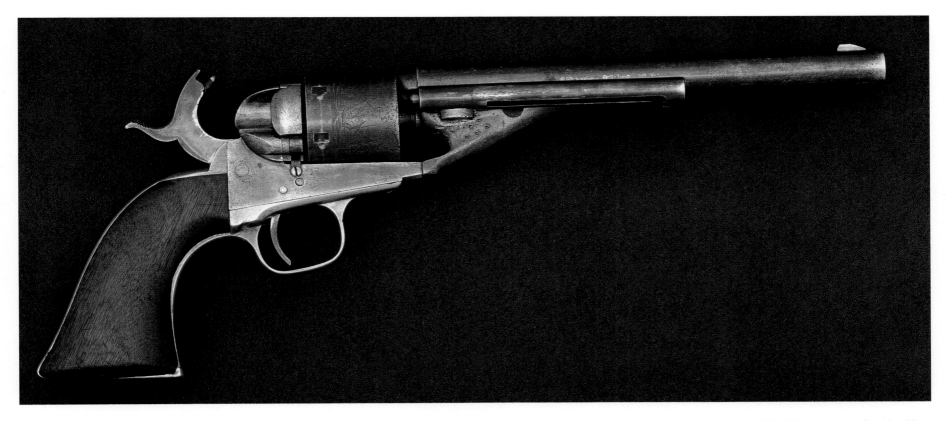

Not regarded as a conversion, the Open Top was Colt's first large-frame cartridge revolver, preceded by the Cloverleaf, four-shot pocket revolver, designed and made as a metallic cartridge breechloader. The new design did away with the need for a breechplate and cut down cylinder, and that might have been the way of the future had the company not been burdened with a vast inventory of Civil War-era percussion parts. Thus it became necessary for Colt's to develop a method of using outdated cap-and-ball frames, cylinders, and barrels in the manufacturing of new cartridge-firing revolvers, this despite the superior design of the Open Top. The Richards-Mason patent then, was simply a means to an end, and while that may take some of the romance out of the cartridge conversion era, it still leaves us with a wonderful variety of gracefully designed Colt percussion revolvers converted to fire metallic cartridges.

Following the 1860 Army, the 1851 Navy was produced in two versions; those built at the factory from percussion inventory and fitted with new conversion parts, and percussion models returned to Colt's for conversion to metallic cartridge. The solid-lug barrels fabricated to the Mason design and used on Hartford-built Navy models quickly distinguish the

This 1861 Navy conversion to .38 caliber centerfire has the cone-type firing pin, which is threaded into the hammer face. This model also has the external gate spring, which is secured to the frame with a small screw. (Dennis Russell Collection)

Typical of percussion conversions of the 1861 Navy, the two-line patent dates are stamped to the right of the COLTS/PATENT mark. The conversion number is stamped on the cylinder and the .36 caliber mark on the frame has either been worn away or deliberately removed to eliminate confusion between the original chambering and the conversion caliber. (Dennis Russell Collection)

two versions from one another. However, some factory Navy conversions were produced by Colt's using only partially completed percussion barrels remaining in inventory, and such examples have the lug bevel scooped out but do not have the loading lever cut at the front of the lug. This comprises a third variation.

Unlike the .44 caliber Army conversions, the .38 caliber Long Colt Navy models were offered in either rimfire or centerfire versions, both with a standard 7-1/2-inch octagonal barrel. For the 1851 Navy, Colt's once again produced two styles of conversion rings, one with an internal spring-tensioned loading gate,

and a second using an external spring. Both variations were seen on rimfire and centerfire models. Those with the external springs are easily recognized as the spring leaf extends downward from the loading gate and is screwed into the side of the frame.

The Navy conversion rings and loading gates were used for the 1861 Navy model as well. (The cylinders were also interchangeable). The new breech ring design was known as the Richards Type III and differed significantly from the conversion rings used on the Second Model 1860 Army. The Army breechplates were milled flat on both sides, whereas

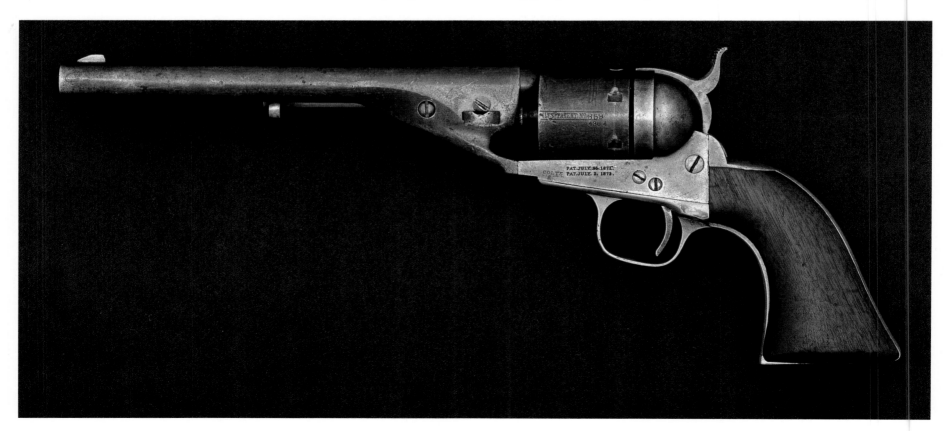

the Type III was flat only on the cylinder breech side while convex on the back. A corresponding concave radius was milled into the face of the recoil shield, allowing the two to seat firmly together. This is seen in the subtle curve of the breech ring and recoil shield on Navy models, particularly when viewed from the right side where the loading gate contours accentuate the lines.

During the early 1870s, the Hartford factory handled approximately 200 original 1851 Navy percussion revolvers returned by private individuals for conversion to metallic cartridge. The price of this service is not known, however, conversions to either .38 Long Colt rimfire or .38 centerfire (the latter

The 1861 Navy was produced in both rimfire and centerfire versions. Pictured at left is a centerfire example with a California pattern holster showing simple border embossing. The centerfire Navy at the right is shown alongside a California pattern open-top holster with incised floral embellishment. Both guns have the external-spring loading gate. The model at the right bears British proof marks. (Roger Muckerheide Collection, holster, George Jackson Collection)

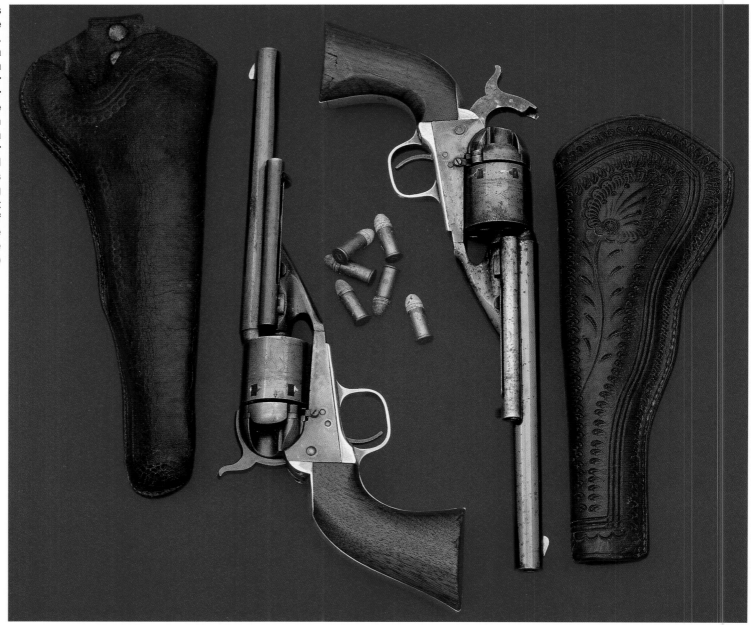

around 1874) were offered. In nearly all such conversions the percussion parts—cylinder and barrel—were reused. The percussion portion of the cylinder was turned down, a new ratchet cut and the chambers bored completely through. The right side of the barrel was milled to accept the Mason ejector, the loading lever channel and screw hole filled, (the plunger hole, however, was left open), the loading lever catch removed, the dovetail filled, and the frame modified to receive the Richards Type III breechplate. This procedure included fitting a double-toothed (f-shaped) hand, necessary to fully engage the new cylinder ratchet and complete the cylinder rotation. This same design was used on 1860 Richards and Richards-Mason conversions.

Factory records indicate that 2,097 Model 1851 and Model 1861 Colt Navy percussion revolvers were returned to Hartford by the U.S. Navy Ordnance Bureau for conversion to the .38 Colt centerfire metallic cartridge.[1]

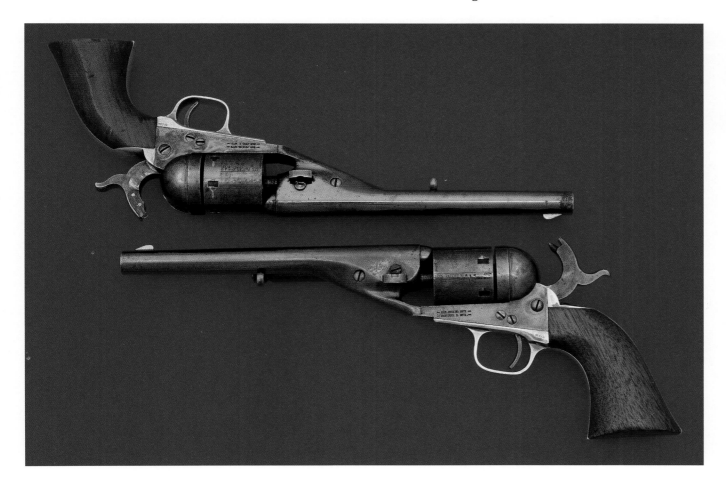

Pictured are two excellent examples of original cartridge conversions on the 1861 Navy. Both have the two-line patent dates with dashes. The rimfire firing pin is clearly shown riveted to the hammer in the top example. (Roger Muckerheide Collection)

Navy-Navy conversion of an 1851 model is stamped with U S N on the buttstrap. (Dow and Russelle Heard Collection)

A Navy-Navy conversion of a percussion model 1851 Navy shows the loading lever plug. The rammer channels were left open to facilitate removal of the barrel using a wooden dowel and mallet. (Dow and Russelle Heard Collection)

The recoil shield channels on 1851 Navy conversions were very deep. The cylinder ratchet is clearly visible in the loading channel. This was typical of all conversions. (Dow and Russelle Heard Collection)

This 1851 Navy-Navy has the iron backstrap and trigger guard typical of the Naval percussion conversions. All Navy-Navy models were chambered for .38 Long Colt centerfire cartridges. This example has the original barrel wedge with spring. (Dow and Russelle Heard Collection)

The left side of the 1851 Navy-Navy conversion shows the addition of the two-line patent dates adjacent to the COLTS/PATENT mark, underneath which is stamped U.S. (Dow and Russelle Heard Collection)

Fitted with the new S-Lug barrel, Type II breechplate and Mason ejector, the 1860 Army had a new lease on life in 1872. The large .44 caliber centerfire model was produced from unnumbered 1860 Army percussion parts remaining in inventory combined with the new barrels, cylinders and conversion parts. The gun is pictured with original boxes of Union Metallic Cartridge Co., and Winchester .44 caliber centerfire cartridges. Also note the dovetailed front sight on this example. (Dow and Russelle Heard Collection)

Percussion conversions were labor-intensive. All repaired surfaces had to be machined and polished to blend in with the original metal of the barrel. (Remember, we're talking about the 1870s, hand tools, primitive belt-driven machinery, no electricity.) Colt's also maintained a small inventory of prepared conversion cylinders, barrels, etc., and some were likely used for contract conversions, in which instance a second set of serial numbers was added to match those of the revolver. The entire gun could also be re-blued or nickel-plated, depending upon the order. And for an additional 75 cents, Colt's

Colt 1860 Army conversion to the Richards-Mason design shows use of the solid-lug barrel, and external-spring hinged loading gate with a retaining screw at the base of the conversion ring. (Dow and Russelle Heard Collection)

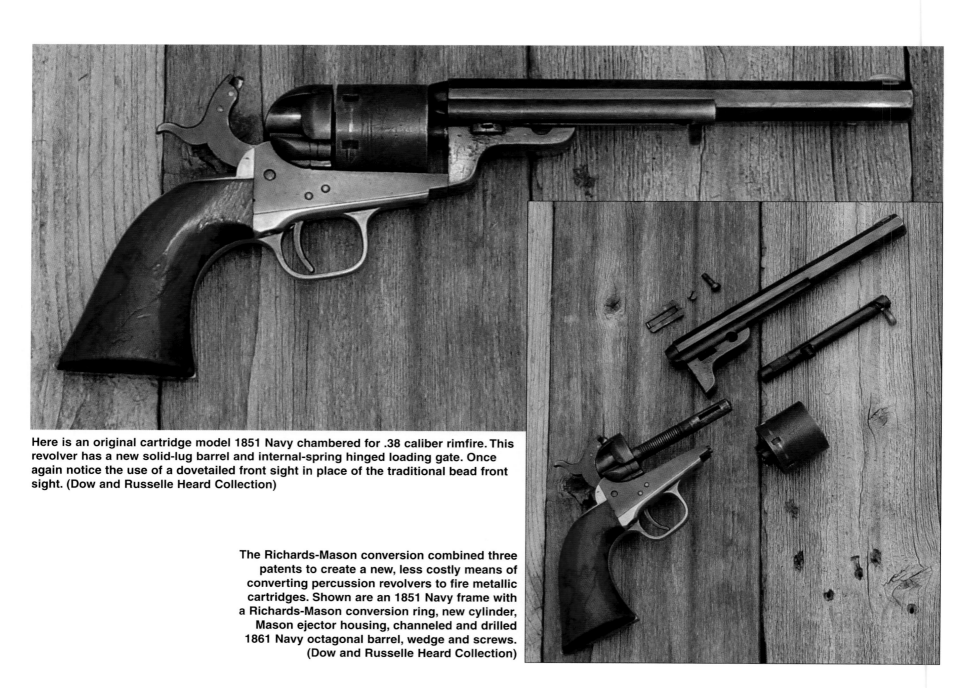

Here is an original cartridge model 1851 Navy chambered for .38 caliber rimfire. This revolver has a new solid-lug barrel and internal-spring hinged loading gate. Once again notice the use of a dovetailed front sight in place of the traditional bead front sight. (Dow and Russelle Heard Collection)

The Richards-Mason conversion combined three patents to create a new, less costly means of converting percussion revolvers to fire metallic cartridges. Shown are an 1851 Navy frame with a Richards-Mason conversion ring, new cylinder, Mason ejector housing, channeled and drilled 1861 Navy octagonal barrel, wedge and screws. (Dow and Russelle Heard Collection)

would supply new wood grips. [2]

In most cases, a percussion conversion (compared to an original metallic cartridge Navy) can be recognized by the loading lever plug, scooped out barrel lug, and filled dovetail that once held the loading lever latch. As previously noted, the plunger channel was not filled. It was left open to facilitate separating the barrel from the frame, which would have been done using the rammer and plunger against the cylinder face. On conversions, if a barrel became difficult to remove, a wooden dowel could be pushed through the plunger opening and tapped with a mallet to exert force against the cylinder and separate the barrel from the frame. It is sometimes amazing how firmly those two small pins at the base of the frame can lodge themselves within the barrel lug.

Between 1871 and 1878 more than 10,000 Colts were converted to .44 caliber and roughly another 6,000 to .38 caliber rimfire and centerfire rounds, the latter, principally 1851 Navy and 1861 Navy models. McDowell noted that there were many variations, often at the expense of correctness, such as 1851 Navy frames fitted with 1861 Navy barrels. There were Navy-Navy conversions, those done under contract for the U.S. Navy using original 1851 Navy percussion revolvers fitted with iron gripstraps; Navy-Army conversions, the same but with brass gripstraps; and civilian Navy models, which could have been a percussion conversion or a new gun manufactured as a cartridge revolver.

The one consistency appears to be that the majority of 1851 Navy conversions had both the Richards and Mason patent dates stamped on the left side of the frame, however, even this practice has variations. Some examples have dashes in front and behind the dates, primarily on original metallic cartridge models, others have only the dates stamped next to, or overlapping the Colt's Patent

In this close-up of the Richards-Mason conversion the concave-convex fit of the breech ring to the frame is evident in the subtle curve revealed by the open loading gate. (Dow and Russelle Heard Collection)

The newly manufactured Mason barrels and ejector housings were easily assembled. The threaded stud on the side of the ejector housing fit into the counter sunk hole just forward of the wedge opening and was secured by a screw passing through the barrel lug from the right side. The new barrels were also channeled to receive the Mason ejector housing. The channel ran from the mid section of the barrel all the way into the forcing cone, thus placing the ejector directly in front of the cylinder. Note the cutout in the ejector housing, which allows the wedge to slip underneath. (Dow and Russelle Heard Collection)

A nickel finish and ivory stocks accent this factory conversion of an 1851 Navy utilizing an old inventory barrel that was dished out for percussion use but not channeled for the loading lever and plunger. (Dow and Russelle Heard Collection)

stamping. In almost all instances these were factory percussion conversions. Navy-Navy models also have U.S. stamped below the patent dates, U.S.N. stamped on the buttstrap, and government inspectors' marks. There are also examples of Navy conversions that have no patent dates on the frame at all, only the Colt's Patent stamping. This, of course, does not take

into account any models converted in the field or guns with non-matching conversion parts, and guns that may have had parts replaced.

Finally, percussion models altered to metallic cartridge with serial numbers below 74000 were stamped with the Type I New York barrel address:
– ADDRESS SAML COLT NEW-YORK CITY –

The Hartford address:

– ADDRESS SAML COLT HARTFORD CT. –

is usually seen on percussion models converted in the serial number range 74000 to 101000. Later percussion models and original cartridge models were stamped with the Type II address:

– ADDRESS COL. SAML COLT NEW-YORK U.S. AMERICA –

The Other Navy

The 1861 Navy has been called the most graceful and beautifully designed revolver ever produced. The size, balance and contours of the 1861 Navy make that assessment hard to dispute. As a cartridge conversion, it was perhaps an even better looking gun.

More than 2,000 were produced, about 400 chambered for .38 caliber rimfire and 1,800 for centerfire rounds, the latter beginning after August 1873 when .38 caliber centerfire cartridges became readily available. Notes R. L. Wilson, "[In addition] about 100 rimfire and 100 centerfire revolvers are estimated to have been field conversions. As a rule of thumb, pistols in the U.S. Navy marked serial number range [approximately numbers 1500 through 9800] are centerfire, as are specimens in the Colt factory produced series in the range number 1400 to 3300. Colt factory produced series revolvers from number 1 through approximately 1400 are usually rimfire."

It is estimated that of the 2,200 Richards-Mason 1861 Navy models built, 1,200 were percussion pistols returned to Colt's for conversion. Serial number ranges for percussion models are below 10356 (most with four digit serial numbers) the majority of which were returned by the U. S. Navy Ordnance Bureau in 1873, 1875, and 1876 for alteration on contract.

Navy-Navy conversions were martially marked, the same as 1851 Navy-Navy models. The left side of

The most elegantly styled of all Colt cartridge conversions is the 1861 Navy. Combining the frame of the 1851 Navy with the barrel design of the 1860 Army, the .36 caliber percussion model evolved into the best cartridge conversion of all. Pictured are a nickel-plated rimfire model and a centerfire model with the external loading gate spring. The serial number range for original metallic cartridge conversions was 1 to 3300. Percussion conversions were produced with serial number ranges to 34000 for civilian models, and 1500 to 10000 for U.S. Navy conversions. (Dow and Russelle Heard Collection)

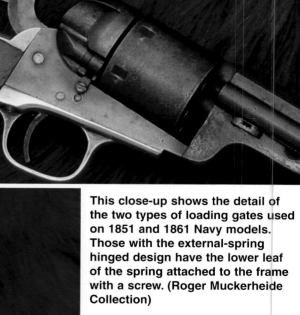

Pictured here are two versions of the 1851 Richards-Mason conversion. The top example is a percussion conversion with the internal-spring hinged loading gate. The second gun is an original cartridge model with solid-lug barrel and external-spring hinged loading gate. (Roger Muckerheide Collection)

This close-up shows the detail of the two types of loading gates used on 1851 and 1861 Navy models. Those with the external-spring hinged design have the lower leaf of the spring attached to the frame with a screw. (Roger Muckerheide Collection)

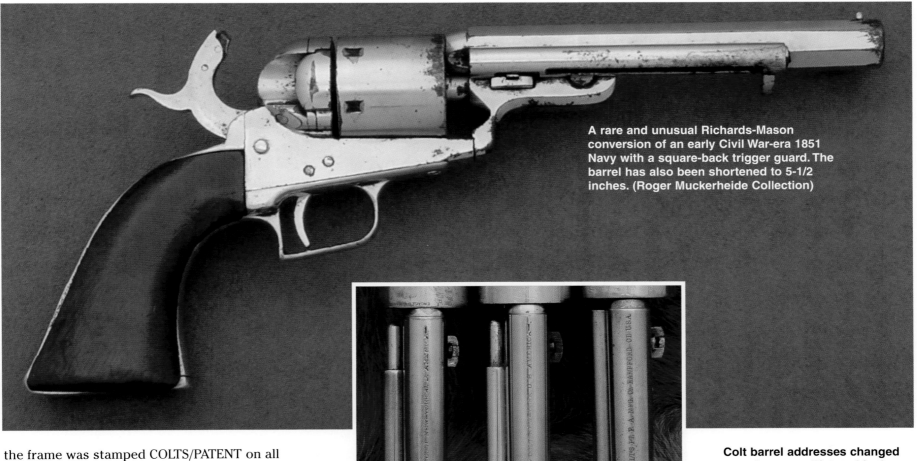

A rare and unusual Richards-Mason conversion of an early Civil War-era 1851 Navy with a square-back trigger guard. The barrel has also been shortened to 5-1/2 inches. (Roger Muckerheide Collection)

Colt barrel addresses changed over the years. Pictured is the Hartford address (right) and two revolvers with the Type II U.S. America address. (Roger Muckerheide Collection)

the frame was stamped COLTS/PATENT on all conversions, and PATENT

PAT. JULY 25, 1871 .–
PAT. JULY 2, 1872 .–

on most examples. As with the 1851 Navy-Navy conversions, the patent dates on 1861 Navy-Navy models were stamped to the immediate right of, or slightly overprinting the COLTS/PATENT marking. On factory produced cartridge models the two-line patent dates were added to the left side of the frame and the COLTS/PATENT stamping eliminated.

The barrel addresses on all 1861 Navy models, regardless of whether a percussion conversion or original metallic cartridge model read:
– ADDRESS COL. SAM͟L COLT NEW-YORK U.S. AMERICA –

The 1861 Navy was easier to manufacture since Colt's had an abundant supply of barrels, thereby eliminating the time and expense of producing new conversion barrels. This had become necessary for the Richards-Mason 1860 Army and 1851 Navy conversions after Colt's remaining Civil War percussion inventory had been depleted.

For 1861 Navy cartridge conversions the barrel loading lever and plunger channels and lever latch dovetail were plugged and machined to blend into the surrounding surfaces. A channel was milled into the right side of the barrel for the ejector housing and a hole drilled and counter-bored for the mounting stud and screw.

The 1861 Navy conversions, like their 1851 counterparts, were produced in three variations: those converted from original percussion revolvers, factory-built examples utilizing remaining percussion inventory, and those converted outside the Colt factory.

As had been the case with the 1851 Navy conversions, both internal-spring and external-spring loading gates were used on the 1861 Navy models, the latter noted by the stem of the spring leaf being screwed into the side of the frame below the gate.

Colt cartridge conversions, beginning with the 1860 Army, utilized a new hand with two fingers (right) in place of the original percussion hand (left).

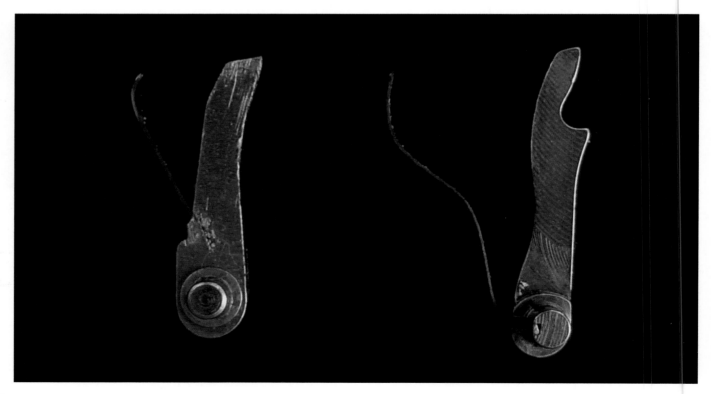

Earlier models were fitted with external springs and succeeded by the internal-spring design as production continued into the 1870s. Colt's exhausted its old inventory of percussion hammers in mid-1872, after which new hammers with distinctive bordered and underlined knurling on their spurs were used on Navy conversions. The new conversions also had a larger diameter hammer screw. All later models bore the two line patent date, which was stamped on the left side of the frame.

The 1861 Navy factory conversions have 7-1/2-inch barrels with slightly crowned muzzles. Field conversions were sometimes fitted with shortened barrels measuring 5-1/2 inches, a popular length for lawmen and those feeling the need to clear leather a little more quickly.

An interesting, and often confusing stamping on most Navy conversions is the .36 caliber mark on the left side of the trigger guard flat, which is a holdover from the percussion era and was not changed when Colt's started producing original .38 caliber cartridge models. There are, however, some examples with .38 stamped over the .36 on the trigger guard.

With both centerfire and rimfire versions produced, it is important to note that there were two different styles of centerfire firing pins in use on the 1861 Navy. The more common is known as the cone-type, which was threaded into the hammer face, whereas the narrow blade-type pin, cut into the hammer face and secured by two lateral rivets, is seen less often. All rimfire conversions were for the civilian market and all military conversions were centerfire.

One of the most popular models of its time, the 1861 Navy remains a highly desirable Colt conversion among present-day collectors. Nickel- or silver-plated examples are prized and engraved and cased models are extremely rare. Most were produced by Schuyler, Hartley and Graham of New York City, and engraved by the legendary Louis D. Nimschke.

The Richards-Mason patents broadened Colt's entire product range by making available a cartridge conversion for every percussion model built from the 1851 Navy to the 1862 Pocket pistols. For those venturing west in the 1870s, a Colt cartridge revolver became one of the most important of all worldly possessions.

[1] *A Study Of Colt Conversions and Other Percussion Revolvers* by R. Bruce McDowell
[2] This was the price charged by Colt's to the U.S. Navy for furnishing new grips on Navy-Navy conversions. The price also included polishing and re-blueing the gripstraps.

The double-toothed (f-shaped) hand was necessary to fully engage the new cylinder ratchet and complete the cylinder rotation. The top tooth would begin to slip off just as the second tooth picked up the next ratchet completing the rotation of the cylinder as the hammer was drawn completely back.

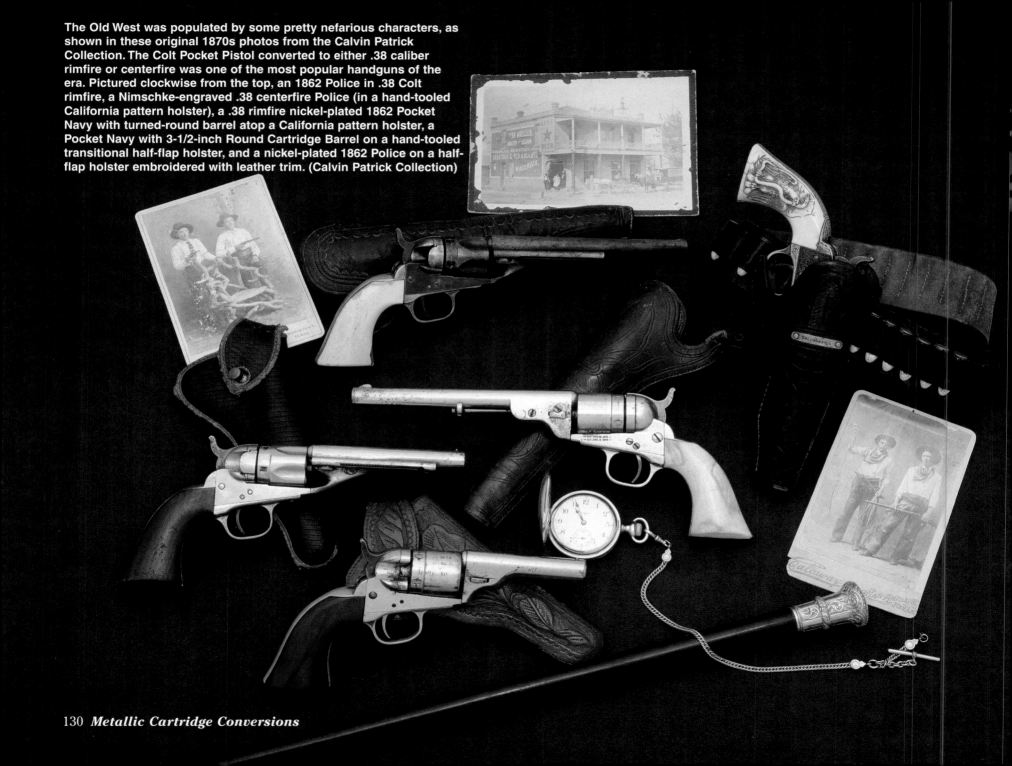

The Old West was populated by some pretty nefarious characters, as shown in these original 1870s photos from the Calvin Patrick Collection. The Colt Pocket Pistol converted to either .38 caliber rimfire or centerfire was one of the most popular handguns of the era. Pictured clockwise from the top, an 1862 Police in .38 Colt rimfire, a Nimschke-engraved .38 centerfire Police (in a hand-tooled California pattern holster), a .38 rimfire nickel-plated 1862 Pocket Navy with turned-round barrel atop a California pattern holster, a Pocket Navy with 3-1/2-inch Round Cartridge Barrel on a hand-tooled transitional half-flap holster, and a nickel-plated 1862 Police on a half-flap holster embroidered with leather trim. (Calvin Patrick Collection)

CHAPTER 8

Small-Frame Colt Breechloaders and Conversions

The Colt Richards and Richards-Mason Pistols

There were certain individuals who, because of their nature or line of work, preferred to carry smaller, lighter revolvers, often concealed in a vest or trouser pocket, or kept close at hand in a small California pattern holster. The cartridge Pocket Pistol became a favorite of gamblers, private detectives, Secret Service and Wells Fargo agents. It was also carried by an endless assortment of nefarious characters and desperados desiring a "hide-away" gun. Yet the Pocket Pistol was a gun no less deadly than its medium-frame counterpart, as most were chambered for .38 rimfire or centerfire cartridges. The Pocket Pistol was also the favored equalizer for women—good women, bad women, and some very bad women. Thus the small, five-shot, .38 caliber Police and Pocket Navy, 1849 Pocket, and even a Paterson conversion or two had

been woven into the fabric of the Old West by the mid 1870s.

R. L. Wilson notes, that for collectors, Colt Pocket Pistols comprise the most exasperating and complex group of cartridge conversions. "Serial number ranges encountered are three—the range of the Pocket Navy, Model 1862 Police, that of the Model 1849 Pocket, and a special range [of new production or original metallic cartridge models] from #1 through approximately #19000. Furthermore, several basic barrel types were employed; loading gates and ejection rods may or may not be present; iron and brass straps were used; barrel and frame markings vary; *et cetera, ad infinitum*."

In the 30 years since R. L. Wilson wrote the above, much additional research has been done. Authors John D. Breslin, William Q. Pirie and David E.

Price, in their new book *Variations of Colt's New Model Police and Pocket Breech Loaders* have determined that there are actually five serial number ranges: Two for newly made guns; plus the ranges for the percussion 1862 Police, Pocket Navy, and 1849 Old Model Pocket.

There are almost as many variations as there are

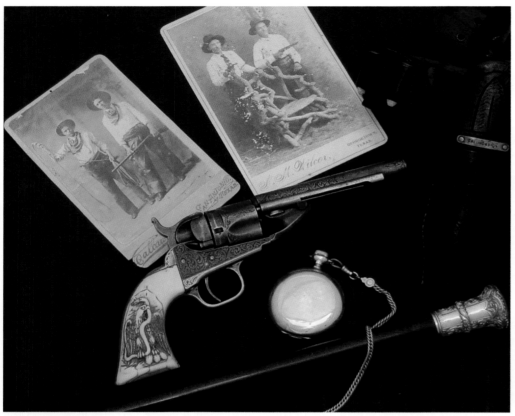

Louis D. Nimschke was responsible for some of the most highly embellished Colt revolvers of the 1870s. This example on an 1862 Pocket Police with a half-fluted percussion cylinder shows the intricate detail applied to the barrel, frame and cylinder. Carved eagle-and-snake ivory grips complete the look of this exquisite period revolver chambered for .38 Colt centerfire cartridges. It is pictured with a hand-tooled holster and belt manufactured by Freund & Bros. (Calvin Patrick Collection)

Here is a June 1875 advertisement for the Colt's .38 Long Police model offered by B. Kittredge & Co. Cincinnati, Ohio. Note that both the gun in the ad and the model shown feature the Police frame with the Navy-style rebated cylinder, which replaced the original half-fluted percussion cylinder on the majority of Police models. The ad clearly shows that the early cartridge pistols and conversions were contemporary with the Peacemaker and later model cartridge revolvers. (Roger Muckerheide Collection)

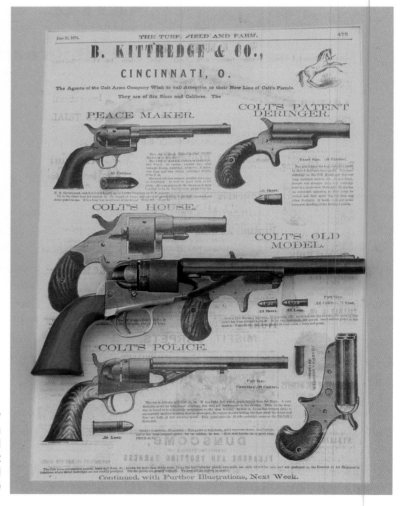

guns, chambered for both rimfire and centerfire rounds, with barrel lengths of 3 inches, 3-1/2 inches, 4-1/2 inches, 5-1/2 inches and 6-1/2 inches.

In all, approximately 32,000 Colt Pocket Pistols were either manufactured as original cartridge models or converted to metallic cartridge at the same time Colt's was manufacturing the 1873 Peacemaker, the New Line Pocket revolver, and the Double Action Lightning models.

"From a review of the above facts," notes Wilson, "it is obvious that Colt's had over produced on percussion parts, and was not about to see these wasted as scrap." Thus Colt's proliferation of breech loading Police and Pocket Pistols extended well beyond any other percussion conversion models.

Small-frame breechloaders and conversions break down into two fundamental categories: Police models, (with ejectors), and Pocket models (without ejectors). This is the way they were referenced in Colt's factory records. Colt's never used the term

Colt's offered the Police cartridge pistols and conversions in three different barrel lengths: 4-1/4, 5-1/2 and 6-1/2 inches. The 6-1/2-inch versions are the most rare. All three examples are early conversions utilizing the original half-fluted percussion cylinder. The new mounting for the Mason patented ejector is clearly seen in the barrel lugs. (Roger Muckerheide Collection)

Early original cartridge models had the **COLTS PATENT** stamping on the left side of the frame. (Roger Muckerheide Collection)

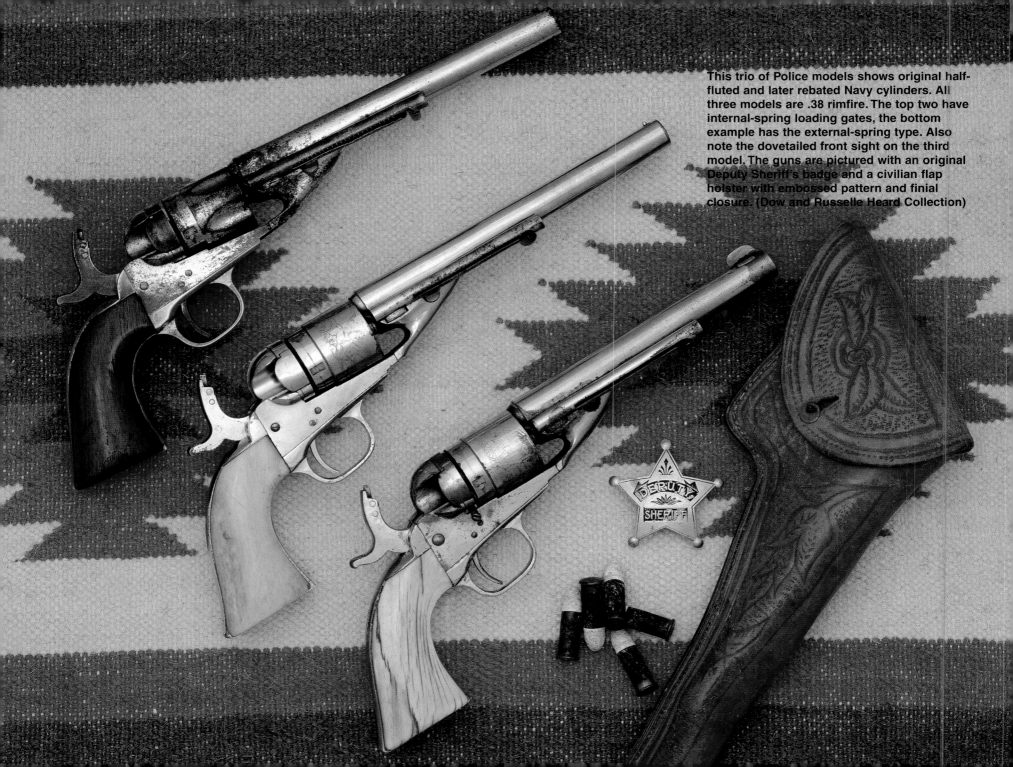

This trio of Police models shows original half-fluted and later rebated Navy cylinders. All three models are .38 rimfire. The top two have internal-spring loading gates, the bottom example has the external-spring type. Also note the dovetailed front sight on the third model. The guns are pictured with an original Deputy Sheriff's badge and a civilian flap holster with embossed pattern and finial closure. (Dow and Russelle Heard Collection)

"conversion." This provides a starting point for cataloging a variety of individual models produced either as new cartridge revolvers or percussion conversions between 1871 and the early 1880s.

The first category, the Police pistol with ejector, was first manufactured in 1871 as a newly made cartridge pistol from modified 1862 Police parts. Initial production used the fluted cylinder, but by mid-1872, the cheaper to manufacture round, roll engraved cylinder replaced the fluted one.

The 1862 Police model was one of Colt's great success stories. A distinctive percussion revolver with a half-fluted, rebated cylinder and 1861 Navy-style barrel, this five-shot, .36 caliber revolver was among the most popular of all Colt percussion models and in the 1870s an ideal candidate for conversion to the metallic cartridge.

Approximately 7,900 original cartridge pistols and 2,900 conversions of previously finished percussion models were produced between 1871 and 1877, and offered in either .38 rimfire or .38 centerfire calibers. The first actual conversions of large stocks of finished percussion pistols took place in 1874.

The majority of Police and Pocket Navy firing pins were of the wedge type (as shown) notched into the hammer and secured by two rivets. The examples pictured are reproductions custom built to original Colt's design by R. L. Millington.

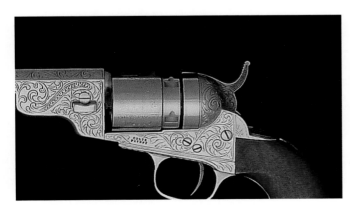

In mid-1872 also, the first Packet models were produced, as newly made cartridge pistols from modified Pocket Navy parts. These had a 4 1/2 inch octagon barrels, with gates, but no ejectors. These initial models were introduced before the receipt of the July 2, 1872 patent, and early examples of original cartridge Police and Pocket Models have thier frames stamped:

COLTS
PATENT

In late 1872, following the issuance of the Richards' and Mason's patents, this was chaned to:

PAT. JULY 25, 1871
PAT. JULY 2, 1872

Two variations of the Richards-Mason Police pistols, an early turned-round percussion barrel and new solid-lug round cartridge barrel. The turned-round barrels acquired a rather distinctive lug profile when converted for metallic cartridge, which quickly distinguishes this model. Both examples have the external hinge-type loading gate. Nickel finishes and ivory grips were quite common on Police models and conversions. Ivory was often chosen by serious pistoleros because it is a porous material and stayed in one's hand better than wood grips. (Dow and Russelle Heard Collection)

The conversion process was almost identical to that of the 1861 Navy. The loading lug and rammer channels were plugged, along with the dovetail for the loading lever latch. Percussion barrels in 4-1/2, 5-1/2, or 6-1/2 inches were milled to fit the Mason patent ejector, the cylinders were cut down and bored through, and the frame fitted with the Richards Type IV conversion ring (for small-frame revolvers).

Interestingly, the majority of Police conversions, those built between 1872 and 1874, were assembled with round, rebated Navy-style cylinders, and

Pocket Navy turned-round barrel and new "solid" cartridge barrels were available in three lengths, 4-1/2, 5-1/2 and 6-1/2 inches. Pictured is a nickel turned-round barrel in 4-1/2 inches, a rare 6-1/2-inch turned-round barrel model, and a later flat-lug original metallic cartridge gun with 4-1/2-inch barrel. All three types of firing pins are also shown, wedge-shaped centerfire, rimfire, and cone-type centerfire. (Roger Muckerheide Collection)

chambered primarily for rimfire cartridges.

The original half-fluted 1862 Police percussion cylinders had proven less adaptable to conversion than the round, rebated Navy cylinders. Additionally, when the supply of original 1862 Police percussion cylinders was exhausted, it was easier and less costly for Colt's to utilize one cylinder design for all Pocket models. With few exceptions, the round, rebated Navy cylinder was then used on *all* late model Pocket Pistol conversions. (This does not include original percussion models sent to Colt's for conversion, in which case the half-fluted cylinder would have been reused).

In mid-1872 the first Pocket models were produced as newly made cartridge pistols modified from 1862 Pocket Navy parts. (The 1862 Pocket Navy percussion model was actually first introduced in 1865, following the great fire that razed most of the Colt factory in February 1864). The 1872 cartridge models had 4-1/2-inch octagon barrels with gates, but no ejectors. These initial octagon-barreled pocket models were numbered in the same serial number range as earlier Police models, but at the beginning of 1873, these pocket models received their own, second, serial number range, starting at serial #1. This range was also used for the 3-1/2-inch "Solid" or S-lug pocket models that were to follow.

Both the Police and pocket models were 5-shot revolvers chambered for either .38 caliber rimfire or .38 Colt Long centerfire cartridges.

The next major event was the introduction of the 3-1/2 inch "Solid Barrel" or Round Cartridge Barrel Pocket Model in early 1875. This revolver was fitted with a 3-1/2 inch barrel, no ejector, or loading gate

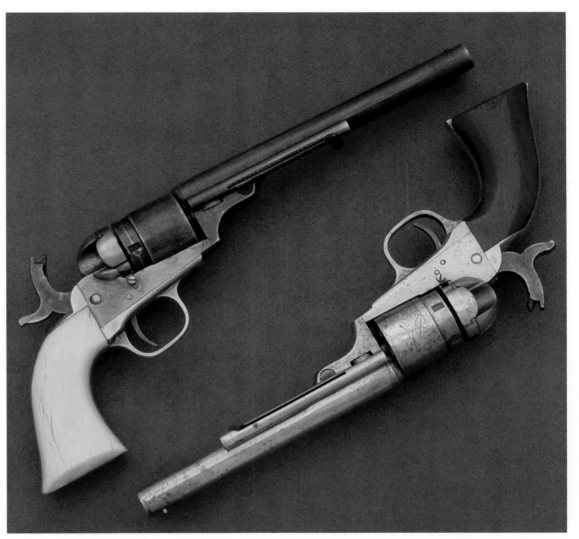

Here is a pair of 1862 Police conversions with 6-1/2- and 5-1/2-inch S-lug Round Cartridge Barrels. The blued example with ivory grips is a centerfire model with wedge-type firing pin; the nickel revolver has the cone-type firing pin. (Roger Muckerheide Collection)

Many Pocket Navy conversions found their way South of the Border. This early1862 Pocket with an octagon barrel in .38 rimfire is fitted with carved Mexican ivory grips and pictured with a quarter-flap Mexican holster featuring yucca or cactus fiber embroidery. (Dow and Russelle Heard Collection)

and built on the 1862 Police, Pocket Navy and 1849 Pocket Pistol frames.

The Model 1849 Pocket was the most popular Colt percussion pistol ever produced, a favorite of miners and sod-busters during the California Gold Rush, the most commonly carried "back-up" gun among Union and Confederate soldiers during the Civil War, and in the 1870s one of the most enduring of all cartridge conversions. The first pistols of this type were made from modified parts as original cartridge guns. About 3,400 original cartridge guns were produced. These were also made as conversions of 1849 Old Model Pocket pistols.

Most conversions in the 1849 serial ranges (approximately #274000 to #328000, an estimated 6,700 guns) were produced from 1876 to 1880. [1] These are extremely interesting specimens because the 1849 was originally chambered for a .31 caliber lead ball, whereas the 1862 Police and Pocket Navy were originally .36 caliber. Yet when they were converted to metallic cartridge, the 1849 models were chambered the same as Police and Navy models, to .38 caliber. During the conversion, the 1849 Model frames were notched (stepped) to permit the use of a new .38 caliber rebated cylinder. All 1849 conversions retained the .31 CAL. stamp on the left side of the trigger guard shoulder, though many were re-stamped with an 8 overprinting the 1.

Showing exceptional Nimschke-style engraving on an early 1862 Police with ivory stocks, this rare example also has a gold washed cylinder. As with the majority of Police models this early example is in .38 caliber rimfire. (Jack Breslin Collection)

A popular model among engravers was the early Pocket Navy with an octagon barrel. Manufactured in 1875, the conversions did not have cartridge ejectors, and were produced without loading gates. An estimated total of 2,000 were assembled with either 3-inch or 4-1/2-inch octagon barrels. Technically, these are Richards conversions, since they do not have the Mason ejector. (Dow and Russelle Heard Collection)

Having been the best-selling Colt percussion model ever built, there was an abundance of 1849 frames and parts on hand well into the 1870s. This was the most compact and lightest of all Pocket Pistol conversions. More reasonably priced than other models, owing to its simple construction (no loading gate or ejector), it became the longest produced Colt cartridge conversion. The distinctive five-shot, 3-1/2-inch Round Cartridge Barrel revolvers were still being sold in the 1880s.

In 1875, all remaining stocks of Pocket Navy models were converted to 3-inch and 4-1/2-inch octagon-barreled pocket models.

The Navy conversions did not have cartridge ejectors, and were produced without loading gates. (Technically, they are Richards conversions, since they do not have the patented Mason ejector and barrel). Thus they differ from those manufactured as cartridge models, which were made with gates. The rebated cylinders bore the traditional roll engraved stagecoach holdup scene, and barrels were marked with the Type II address. Total production was 2,000 pistols including those with 3-inch barrels and a fairly large number of conversions of previously finished engraved pistols.

The next major development was the introduction of a Police model featuring the Mason cartridge ejector and an octagon percussion barrel turned round. It was produced in both .38 Colt Long centerfire and rimfire versions, and available with 4-1/2-, 5-1/2-, or 6-1/2-inch barrels. With the octagon barrel turned round, a distinctive barrel lug contour, and Mason ejector housing, the round barrel Police pistols are among the most desirable of all Richards-

Mason Pocket models. It is estimated that 4,500 were manufactured, primarily as original cartridge pistols, although some barrels were used on conversions of 1862 Police.

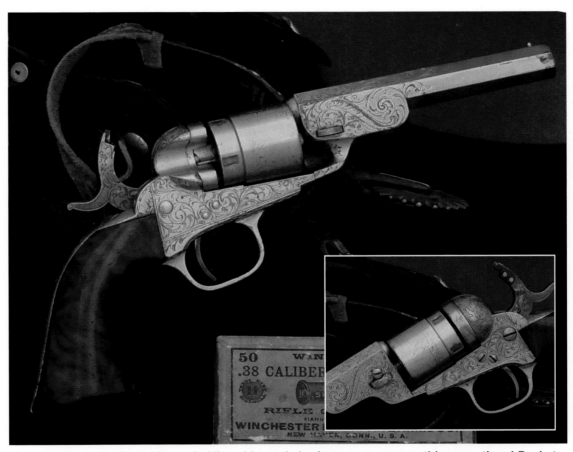

Engraved by L. D. Nimschke, or in Nimschke style by factory engravers, this exceptional Pocket Navy with a 4-1/2-inch octagon barrel exhibits the fine attention given the assembly of cartridge conversion Colts. Features to note are the partially obscured "dog's head" hammer engraving near the rimfire firing pin, the special COLTS PATENT engraving, and .36 CAL. stamp added to the trigger guard just below the shoulder on the left side of the gun. The small V stamped on the front of the trigger guard indicates a factory engraved gun.

One version that left no one in doubt as to its origins was the new Round Cartridge Barrel Police Pistol with ejector and loading gate. Produced at the end of the conversion period, this compact, Five-shot revolver was fitted with a new production S-Lug, or "Solid" barrel available in lengths of 5-1/2, and 6-1/2

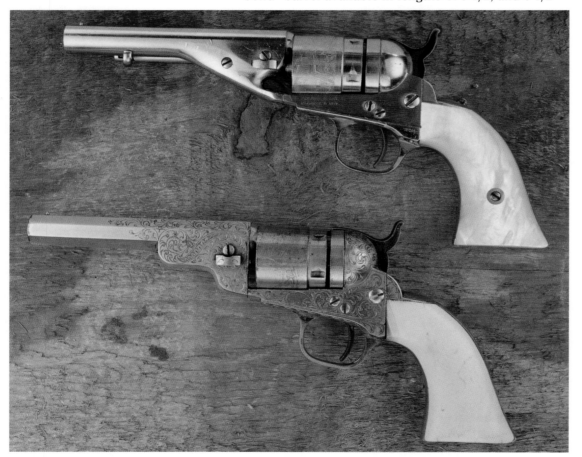

This is another example of the early Pocket Navy with Nimschke engraving, octagon barrel and ivory stocks. This example also bears the small V stamped on the front of the trigger guard. Above is a nickel-plated Police conversion with ivory stocks. Note the two-line patent stamping without dashes. (Photo courtesy R. L. Wilson)

inches, and chambered almost exclusively for .38 centerfire. All Round Cartridge Barrel models were stamped with the

COLT'S PT.F.A. MFG.Co
HARTFORD CT. U.S.A.

barrel address and the Richards-Mason patent dates were stamped on the left side of the frame. Total production was about 1,500 guns, making it the scarcest of the small-frame models. About one third were made as cartridge guns, while the balance were converted from finished 1862 percussion Police pistols.

Production of small-frame conversion parts spanned two distinct periods: between 1871 and 1875, and again as percussion inventory began to dwindle, from 1877 to 1879. Models produced throughout both periods are distinguished by a number of specific characteristics. All Police conversions had percussion barrels with the loading lever channels and lever catch dovetail plugged and refinished to blend with the surrounding surfaces. These were produced from existing percussion inventory. Occasionally, octagon-turned round barrels or new S-lug "Solid" barrels were used to convert percussion Police pistols, possibly when the original percussion barrel was spoiled, or when a longer length was wanted.

Barrel addresses on both Police and Navy models were either the single-line address:

ADDRESS COL. SAMₗ COLT NEW-YORK U.S. AMERICA.

or original two-line address:

ADDRESS SAMₗ COLT
HARTFORD CT.

The new S-lug round cartridge barrels or turned-round barrels bore the later two-line address:

COLT'S PT. F.A. MFG. Co
HARTFORD. CT. U.S.A.

A fourth variation covers those models made for England, which bear the London address:

ADDRESS SAMl COLT
LONDON

Solid-lug Round Cartridge Barrels were produced after the supplies of percussion 1862 Pocket Police and Pocket Navy barrels were exhausted. They were 3-1/2 inches for the Pocket Pistols, and 5-1/2- and 6-1/2-inch lengths for the Police Models.

Turned round barrels were originally octagon percussion barrels re-machined by Colt's for the cartridge Police pistols and offered in barrel lengths of 4-1/2, 5-1/2 and 6-1/2 inches. It is not exactly clear why Colt's chose to do this, since it was quite a machining job. It could be assumed this was done to deplete the remaining percussion barrel inventory by making them look similar to the new modified 1862 Police barrels. [2]

The design of Pocket Pistol loading gates, when loading gates were fitted, followed those of the Richards-Mason 1851 Navy and 1861 Navy, using both internal and external spring designs. Breechplates also followed the large-frame configuration, with a convex/concave fit to the recoil shield, and replacement of the single-tooth percussion revolver

This is an engraved 1862 Police conversion with a Navy-style rebated cylinder. It is chambered for .38 centerfire with a wedge-type firing pin. (Ex John B. Solley III Collection. Photo courtesy R. L. Wilson)

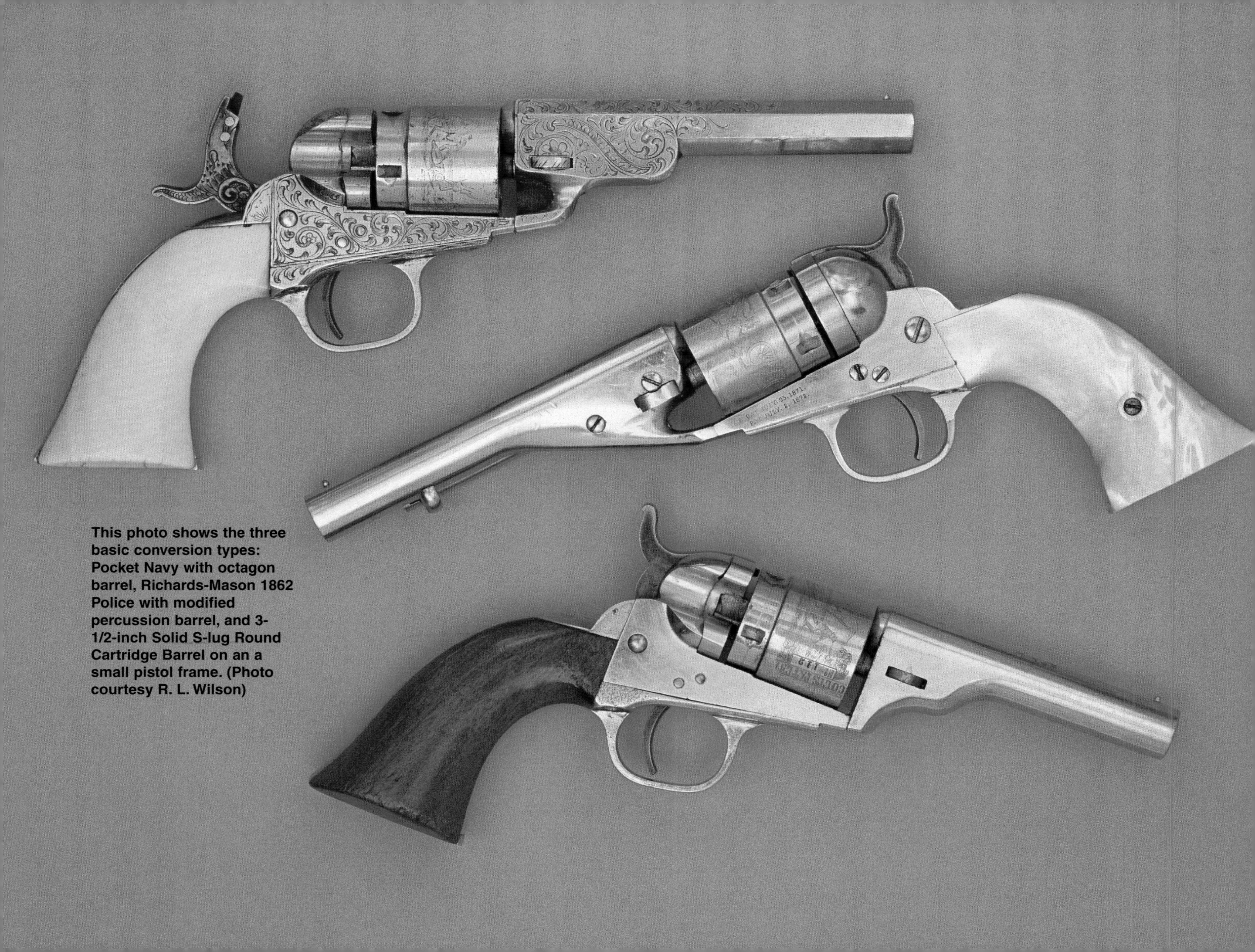

This photo shows the three
basic conversion types:
Pocket Navy with octagon
barrel, Richards-Mason 1862
Police with modified
percussion barrel, and 3-
1/2-inch Solid S-lug Round
Cartridge Barrel on an a
small pistol frame. (Photo
courtesy R. L. Wilson)

Here is a variety of small-frame conversions showing different barrel lengths and finishes. At the top left is a 6-1/2-inch model with a rebated Navy cylinder, below, a nickel-plated model with a 5-1/2-inch barrel and carved eagle ivory stocks; at right, a pair of 3-1/2-inch barrel conversions one nickel with ivory grips, and one blued finish with walnut grips. (Roger Muckerheide Collection. Knife and mercantile sign George Jackson Collection)

Pocket Pistols were intended for easy concealment and this round of Colts certainly fits the bill. Clockwise, a rare, early 3-inch octagon-barrel Pocket Navy conversion without loading gate; a 3-1/2-inch Round Cartridge Barrel model on an 1849 frame; a 4-1/2-inch Pocket with octagon barrel; a nickel finish 4-1/2-inch original cartridge Pocket with octagon barrel, external-spring loading gate and ivory grips; a 4-1/2-inch original cartridge pocket with internal-spring loading gate; a 4-1/2-inch nickel finish early model Pocket Navy conversion with factory engraving; and a 3-inch nickel finish Pocket Navy conversion without loading gate. (Roger Muckerheide Collection)

hand with the new double-tooth conversion hand.

Pocket model hammers were cut to seat either a rimfire pin on the left side of the hammer, or a wedge-type pin notched into the hammer face for centerfire models. The firing pins on both versions were secured to the hammer by two rivets. On a few centerfire conversions a cone-type firing pin screwed into the hammer face was also used, however, the wedge-type is the most commonly seen. The majority of Pocket Pistols, however, appear to have been chambered for rimfire cartridges.

As previously mentioned, most Pocket Pistols had both patent dates stamped on the left side of the frame, but pistols produced in 1871 and the first part of 1872 bore the markings:

COLTS

PATENT

Conversions of engraved percussion pistols also retained this marking to prevent grinding away the engraving. On later production Pocket models with the 4-1/2-inch barrel and 1862 Police and original metallic cartridge models, the Richards-Mason patent dates are stamped without the dashes:

PAT. JULY 25. 1871.

PAT. JULY 2. 1872.

On turned-round barrel Pocket Navy models and on all solid-lug barrel models, the patent dates appear with the dashes in front of and behind each date, however, without the period after 1871.

PAT. JULY 25. 1871 -

PAT. JULY 2. 1872. -

It should be further noted that on some early

The most popular series of Colt cartridge conversions was produced into the early 1880s. Pictured are 3-1/2-inch Round Cartridge Barrel models built on 1849 Pocket frames. Nickel finishes and ivory grips were common. (Dow and Russelle Heard Collection)

conversions of Model 1862 Police pistols with ejectors and loading gates, that the top patent date stamp was the same as seen on early Single Action Army revolvers [3].

PAT. SEPT. 19. 1871.
PAT. JULY 2. 1872.

As with the turned round Navy barrels, there is no documented explanation for this change in manufacturing. The SEPT. 19. 1871 patent date appeared on early Peacemakers approximately within the serial number range of 25 to 22000, which according to *Colt's Dates Of Manufacture* by R. L. Wilson would cover the period from 1873 to 1876.

Police and Pocket Pistols, perhaps by the nature of their smaller size, were more often engraved and plated with nickel or silver than large frame Colt conversions. Some of the finest embellishments by master engravers such as Gustave Young and Louis D. Nimschke appear on Colt Police and Pocket Navy models, both from the percussion era and throughout the 1870s and 1880s. [4]

Small-frame pistols rang down the curtain on the cartridge conversion era, being both the last percussion models introduced by Colt's and the last to be converted for the metallic cartridge.

By the mid 1880s, the American frontier had for the most part been settled, though it was still the Wild West and would remain so into the early 1900s. During the period from 1872 to 1885, however, vast improvements in the design of firearms by Colt's, Smith & Wesson, and Remington had finally closed the books on one of the greatest chapters in the history of the gun. The era of the cartridge

This photo shows a set of Round Cartridge Barrel models with 3-1/2-inch barrels on 1849 Pocket frames. The top two models are centerfire with wedge-type firing pins; the bottom example is a rimfire. (Roger Muckerheide Collection)

conversion was over. The guns that had won the West were traded away, wrapped in oiled cloth and put on shelves, discarded or forgotten—left to await their rediscovery by another generation in another century.

[1] The Book of Colt Firearms by R. L. Wilson
[2] A Study Of Colt Conversions and Other Percussion Revolvers by R. Bruce McDowell
[3] Ibid
[4] The Gustave Young and L. D. Nimschke styles influenced Colt's factory and independent engraving throughout the percussion era and well into the 1870s. Nimschke's style in particular became the most prevalent in the post-Civil War period as he continued to work up until the late 19th century.

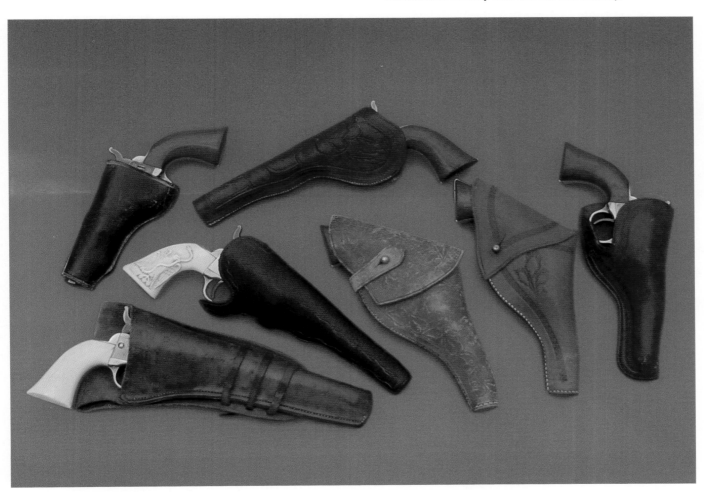

Many holsters were produced to fit Pocket Pistols, from the traditional California pattern and full-flap civilian military-style, to small open-top and custom holsters designed for concealment or quick draw. (Roger Muckerheide Collection)

Colt's 1871-72 Open Top was a unique design preceding the introduction of the Richards and Richards-Mason cartridge conversions. Chambered for .44 Henry rimfire cartridges, the Open Top was the first production cartridge revolver manufactured by Colt's Patent Fire-Arms Mfg. Co. A total of approximately 7,000 were produced from 1871 to 1873. This example with the external-spring loading gate is pictured with a saddle, pummel bag-holster and an elaborately decorated "Mexican loop" pattern holster. (Dow and Russelle Heard Collection)

CHAPTER 9

The 1871-72 Open Top

Colt's First Production Cartridge Revolvers

E very Colt cartridge revolver developed throughout the early 1870s bears the signature of either Charles B. Richards or William Mason. In the case of the 1871-72 Open Top, Colt's first new model cartridge revolver, both Mason and Richards had a hand in the development of the short-lived .44 rimfire model.

Confusion and misconception have always surrounded this historic Colt six-gun because the Open Top was neither a transitional model nor a cartridge conversion, it was an original design intended by William Mason to be produced as an original cartridge model. Its introduction preceded that of the Richards-Mason percussion conversions, and both types were produced concurrently in 1872-73.

Colt's experimented with several variations of the Open Top design, including models chambered for .44 centerfire, .38 centerfire, and .32 rimfire cartridges, the latter two variations often referred to as "Baby Open Top" revolvers, as they were assembled on a smaller frame, about the size of a Police or Pocket Navy model.

Although William Mason and C. B. Richards built a number of experimental Open Tops in Colt's model room, the only example put into production was chambered for the .44 Henry rimfire cartridge. The question was posed in an earlier chapter as to the reason Colt's chose this round over .44 caliber centerfire cartridges. At the time (1871) there was an abundance of .44 Henry rimfire ammunition in circulation because the Henry Rifle and the Winchester Model 1866 were both very popular on the western frontier. Thus with the Open Top

chambered for .44 rimfire, one type of cartridge could be used for both rifle and pistol. While this appears to be a logical explanation, it becomes somewhat paradoxical, as in less than a year Colt's had available the Richards 1860 Army conversion chambered for .44 centerfire, the cartridge preferred by the U.S. military. The explanation, as McDowell interpreted it, was that Oliver Winchester's .44 Henry rimfire cartridges were more readily available, thus providing a ready market for a .44 caliber rimfire revolver. Ultimately, it becomes a moot point as the Open Top was out of production by the summer of 1873, whereas the Richards and Richards-Mason Army conversions chambered for .44 centerfire cartridges remained in production until 1878.

On the other hand, the .38 caliber rimfire cartridge had a rather lengthy run, as Colt's continued to offer Richards-Mason conversions and original metallic cartridge models of the 1851 Navy and 1861 Navy, 1862 Police and Pocket models chambered for rimfire or centerfire cartridges until the early 1880s. The Open Top then, was the only production casualty of the cartridge conversion era—an ironic turn of events since it wasn't a conversion at all but an entirely new model. It would be unfair to call the 1871-72 Open Top a failure. The limited production of approximately 7,000 examples has made it a highly collectible model today.

At a glance, the Open Top resembles the Richards-Mason Army, fitted with the later solid S-lug barrel, but can be quickly distinguished by the integral rear sight cast into the top of the barrel at the breech and the full-length non-rebated cylinder.

The Open Top did not require a conversion ring as the breech area was machined directly from the recoil shield. As such, the loading gate was now a separate assembly mounted to the frame by a screw at the base of the gate. Similar to the Richards and Richards-Mason cartridge conversions, 1871-72 Open Tops utilized both the internal and external loading gate spring designs, the latter noted by the bottom of the spring leaf being screwed to the frame just above the trigger screw.

The general configuration of the Open Top frame was that of the 1860 Army, however without the step required by the front section of the old Army-style rebated cylinder. All factory-produced models had 7-1/2-inch barrels, although a number are seen with 5-3/8-inch or 5-1/2-inch barrels. The shortened barrel

This is a typical Open Top with nickel finish and ivory grips. It is shown with a California pattern holster embellished with ornate hand tooling. (Roger Muckerheide Collection)

was favored by frontier lawmen as it allowed for a quicker draw, sometimes the difference between life and death in the untamed cow towns of the 1870s. Colt's, however, did not offer short barrels, thus any Open Top with a barrel length other than 7-1/2 inches would have been modified either by the owner or a gunsmith.

Most of the parts for the Open Top frame and lock mechanism were interchangeable with the Richards-Mason 1860 Army conversions, and the Mason-style cartridge ejector was used as well. There were two versions of the Open Top, distinguished principally by the size of the grips. On early models, the shorter 1851 Navy-size grips were used with brass gripstraps, whereas in later production the heftier 1860 Army stocks were fitted with steel gripstraps. Of course there are variations. Often at Colt's whatever was at hand was used.

There was some degree of consistency in Open Top factory stampings. All models had .44 CAL stamped on the left triggerguard shoulder[1], barrel addresses were:

The Open Top was often nickel-plated and a few examples featured heavy embellishment and carved ivory grips. (Nickel gun Roger Muckerheide Collection and engraved gun George Jackson Collection)

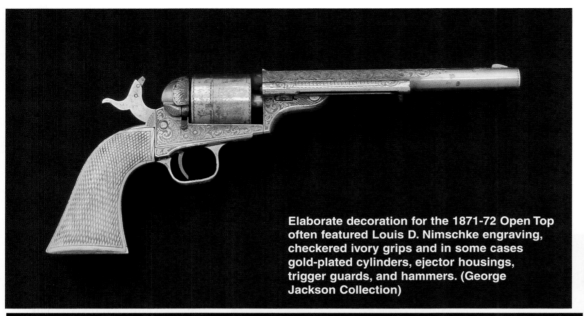

Elaborate decoration for the 1871-72 Open Top often featured Louis D. Nimschke engraving, checkered ivory grips and in some cases gold-plated cylinders, ejector housings, trigger guards, and hammers. (George Jackson Collection)

ADDRESS COL. SAML COLT NEW-YORK U.S. AMERICA — on all but very late production pieces. The last examples bore the
COLT'S PT. F.A. MFG. CO. HARTFORD. CT. U.S.A.
address. And all Open Top pistols had the
COLTS
PATENT
stamp on the left side of the frame.

Although the Open Top was a new design, it suffered the same disadvantages as earlier Colt

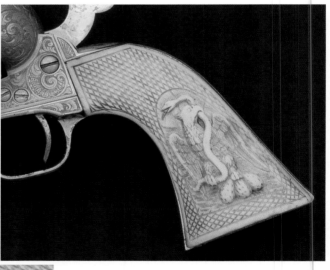

This superb example of Nimschke-style engraving on an Open Top also displays carved eagle-and-snake checkered ivory grips and gold-plated cylinder and hammer. Most examples have survived 130 years because they saw little or no use. (George Jackson Collection)

revolvers: an open frame and separate barrel pinned to the cylinder arbor. Stiff competition from Remington, which had introduced a solid-frame revolver back in 1858, compounded by the U.S. Ordnance Department's rejection of the Open Top as a military sidearm, finally compelled the company to abandon Samuel Colt's original design and develop a solid-frame model that would be the equal of the Remington.

As R. L. Wilson noted in *The Book Of Colt Firearms* "Bearing in mind the rejection of the Open Top by the U.S. Ordnance Department, Colt's engineers, particularly William Mason, worked feverishly to develop the successor to the Open Top…The Single Action Army was a natural evolution by combination of the best design features of the percussion, conversion and Open Top models with the necessary alterations dictated by military needs and the properties of the metallic cartridge ammunition. In 1872 the Colt Peacemaker was adopted by the U.S. Army, following a vigorous and highly competitive series of tests." The Open Top's fate was sealed.

Although cartridge conversion models, combining old percussion inventory with new barrels and cylinders, continued for another decade, the Single Action Army was the start of a new chapter in Colt's history. The cartridge conversion had seen its day.

Or had it?

[1] This was often removed on engraved examples.

The 1873 Single Action Army brought Open Top production to a hasty conclusion, and rang down the curtain on the cartridge conversion era. The legendary Colt Peacemaker remained in production from the time of its introduction in 1873 until 1940! It was brought back in 1956 and contemporary Colt SAA models are still being built to this day. (Dow and Russelle Heard Collection)

R. L. Millington's superb craftsmanship and attention to authentic detail are shown in these Richards-Mason cartridge conversions. Both the 1860 Army and 1862 Police are engraved in the Louis D. Nimschke style and lightly antiqued. The antique russet holster is by Classic Old West Styles.

CHAPTER 10

Modern Reproductions

Recreating the Past

There's nothing like a brand new gun... except a brand new old gun While it's a bit of a contradiction, a demand has arisen over the past half dozen years for reproductions of Colt, Remington and other percussion-era metallic cartridge conversions. The craft of authentically reproducing these historic six-guns goes back almost two decades, to the early 1980s when gunsmith Kenny Howell began restoring original cartridge conversion for filmmakers and private collectors.

Recalls Howell; "I needed parts that were no longer available so I made them myself. I was a tool and die maker by trade, so I set up the tooling and molds to reproduce whatever pieces I needed to complete a repair or restoration. Then it occurred to me, I could take one of the Italian percussion revolvers and make it into an authentic-looking cartridge conversion. The first one I did was an 1851 Navy. That was almost 20 years ago."

Since then, Howell has built more than 300 Colt reproductions, and about a dozen 1858 Remington conversions. While many of them have been based on Uberti and Colt Second and Third Generation percussion models, Howell has also built a number of guns from scratch, mostly those used in films demanding absolute authenticity. Howell made three copies of an 1871-72 Open Top for use by Tom Selleck in the film *Crossfire Trail*, and a fourth built for the author's private collection.

"I made the molds and dies to produce that gun to the original specifications, including the Navy size grips and gripstrap seen on the early Open Top models." Howell said. He even hand-carved the ivory stocks for all four examples.

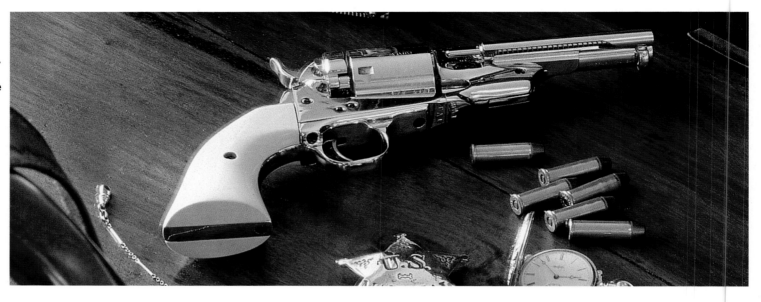

Piece by piece, a reproduction cartridge conversion is laid out on a copy of the Richards patent. Recreating the past means building guns with the same style parts as Colt's used 130 years ago. This custom Richards-style Colt was built by Dave Anderson in 1997.

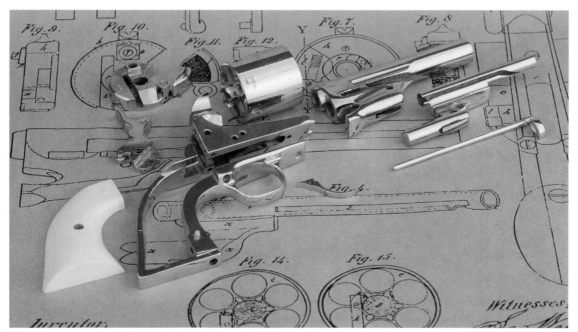

Howell has built a number of Richards and Richards-Mason conversions using Second Generation Colts and produced a limited series of guns for Colt Blackpowder Arms using the Third Generation 1851 Navy and 1860 Army. "There were 60 in total," he said. "Twenty Richards 1860 Army models and 40 Richards-Mason 1851 Navy models. That was in 1995." When those guns appear on the secondary market they command upwards of $1,500.

Howell's guns have also appeared in Tom Selleck's epic Civil War drama, *Last Stand at Saber River*, in the film ***Wyatt Earp***, starring Kevin Costner, the 1982 Australian film *The Man From Snowy River*, and in *The Wild, Wild West*, starring Will Smith and Kevin Kline. Howell is currently producing guns for Tom Selleck's remake of the 1970 film *Monte Walsh*, originally starring Lee Marvin and Jack Palance.

With a busy film schedule, Howell still manages

In the late 1990s, California gunsmith Dave Anderson produced a series of production Colt cartridge conversions. He also built custom revolvers for individuals and for use in films. This striking pair of Colt Pocket Pistols was among his finest work. The guns are shown with an original embossed civilian flap holster and a Wah-Maker western vest.

Spokane, Washington gunmaker John Gren was one of the earliest builders of Colt cartridge conversions. This pair of Second Generation Colt 1860 Army models exhibits Gren's unusual style of combining First Model Richards and Richards-Mason designs in his conversions. The hammer face has been ground flat, the conversion ring has a rebounding firing pin and integral Richards Type I rear sight, but is otherwise of the Richards-Mason dimensions. (Dennis Russell Collection)

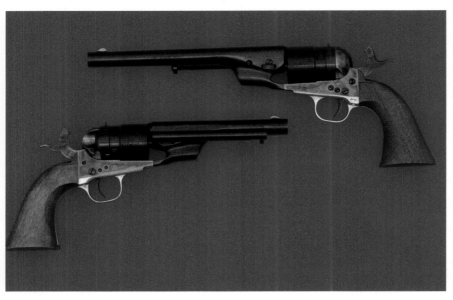

The two most common John Gren cartridge conversions are the 1860 Army and 1851 Navy. Both examples shown were done on Second Generation Colts. (Dennis Russell Collection)

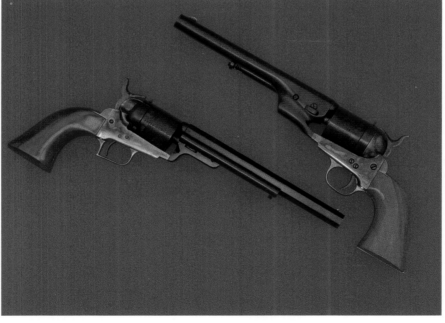

to produce a handful of custom-built conversions for individual customers and plans to increase production in 2003 with a line of Open Tops, 1860 Army, 1851 Navy and 1858 Remington conversions, which will all be handcrafted by Howell and the R&D Gunshop in Beloit, Wisconsin.

In The Beginning

One of the earliest reproduction conversions, recalls Howell, was a gun called *The Legal Defender*. "It was produced as a kit back in the 1960s, and came with the parts and instructions to convert an 1851 Navy for .38 S&W. Years later, gunsmith John Gren based an entire series of handcrafted conversions on that design, which was a combination of the First Model Richards-style hammer and floating firing pin with the Richards-Mason design breechplate and cylinder. They were pretty neat and when they first came out in the early 1980s they inspired a lot of other gunsmiths." Most of Gren's guns, which were built using Second Generation Colts, are now in private collections and rarely appear on the secondary market.

One gunsmith encouraged by Gren and Howell is R. L. Millington, who has refined the art of building authentic reproductions with his popular antique finishes and L.D. Nimschke-style engraving.

Millington developed his own formula for creating antique reproductions of great 19th century American revolvers—pistols so authentic in detail and finish that most casual

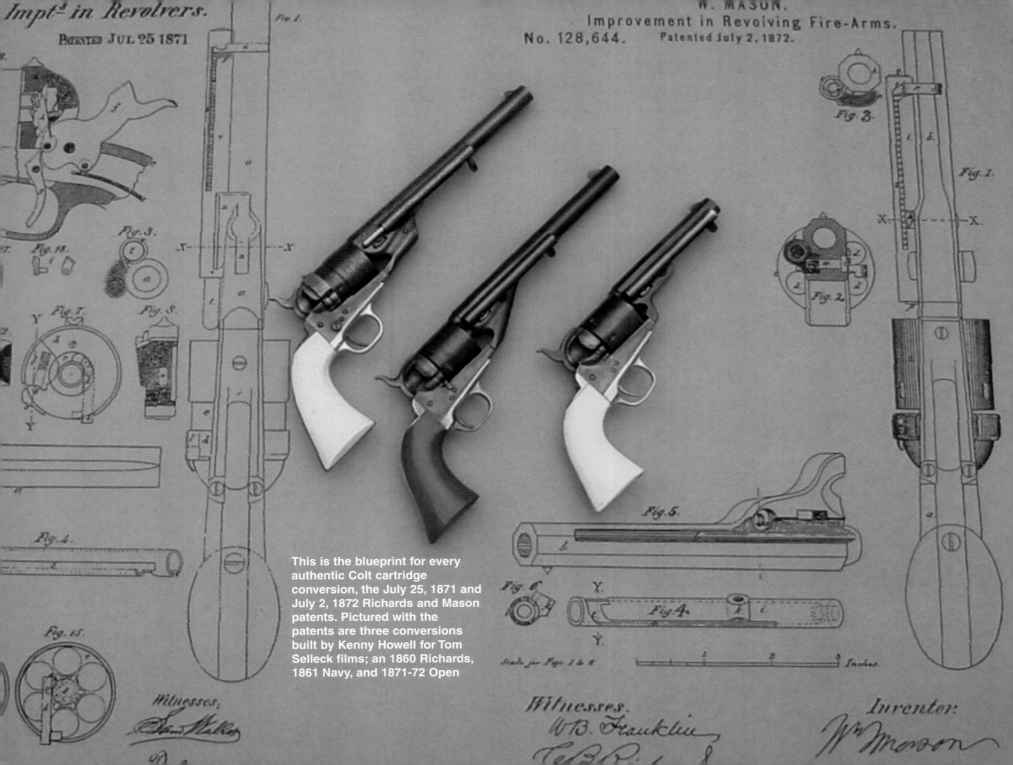

This is the blueprint for every authentic Colt cartridge conversion, the July 25, 1871 and July 2, 1872 Richards and Mason patents. Pictured with the patents are three conversions built by Kenny Howell for Tom Selleck films; an 1860 Richards, 1861 Navy, and 1871-72 Open

observers and more than a few learned professionals have a difficult time telling a Millington reproduction from an original. Of course there are a few telltale features including serial numbers that belie the gun's apparent originality.

Over the last five years Millington has mastered the aging process with a formula he created. "I use a bluing from Brownells called Dicropan 'IM' and I found out that if you don't follow their steps and you don't do it right you come out with what I've got for the finish!" said Millington. The finish looks authentically old, but it's not as easy at it sounds. "I've done a lot of experimenting with bluing to get just the right colors," stresses Millington, and he adds that the brass backstraps and trigger guards on Colts and Remingtons are even harder to authentically age. "There's a nice dull finish you see on the old Model 66 Winchesters, and that's what I am trying to capture in my process," he said.

The total aging process (which is an additional charge on Millington's Colt and Remington cartridge conversions), involves removing the Italian proof marks, and on occasion, slightly reshaping the frame or backstrap to obtain dimensions as close as possible to the originals, with which manufacturers often take liberties for the sake of cost. Stocks have to be aged as well, and when a truly antique look is requested, flat spots, holster-wear and even metal flaking and rust are worked into the gun's finish. The results can vary from a gun with some wear to one that appears to have been found wrapped in an oilcloth since the 1880s.

While the antique finishes are what first attract most people to Millington's guns—wondering if they are originals—the workmanship is his real forte. The guns are hand-built from Colt and Italian made black powder reproductions.

He started by converting 1858 Remingtons to .45 Colt in 1995. "I had pictures of original conversions and I had a modern black powder cap-and-ball reproduction, so I decided to try and make one," Millington said. "I did it for myself to use in single-

Kenny Howell has been building authentic conversions for films since the 1980s. Pictured are Colts from a number of films and a prototype Remington conversion Howell plans to put into limited production in 2003. At the top is Tom Selleck's First Model Richards from *Last Stand At Saber River;* below is an 1851 Navy seen in a number of films. It is Howell's personal gun used in SASS competition. Next, the 1871-72 Open Top carried by Selleck in *Crossfire Trail*. Finally an 1861 Navy conversion and the Remington prototype.

action shooting, and then someone asked if I could make one for them. That's basically how it got started."

Most of his customers are cowboy action shooters, "...they want an authentic-looking gun," he said. "I have duplicated the Remington factory conversion exactly as it was done in 1868, with the exception of the caliber which was originally .46 rimfire."

In building his reproductions, Millington follows the original Remington pattern, which is a five-shot cylinder (that he makes himself from solid bar stock), no loading gate, and an ejection rod housing dovetailed into the right barrel lug, and held in place by a screw and a cutout in the loading lever. Unlike Colt conversions, the early Remington ejector rod was not spring-loaded, and it had to be retracted manually after pushing each shell casing out of the chamber. This little oddity adds even more authenticity to Millington's conversions, and as with the originals, the ejector is not standard on the Remington Army. The original 1868 order for 4,574 New Army .46 caliber rimfire conversions did not include the hand ejector. It became a standard feature of the later Remington New Model Navy factory conversions.

In order to make an authentic-looking reproduction, Millington strips the guns (usually Uberti 1858 Remingtons) down to the individual parts. The first step is to dovetail the back of the frame where the cylinder butts up against the recoil shield. This is to make room for the new backplate, which slips in between the back of the frame and the cylinder. The backplate is dovetailed in, and there is

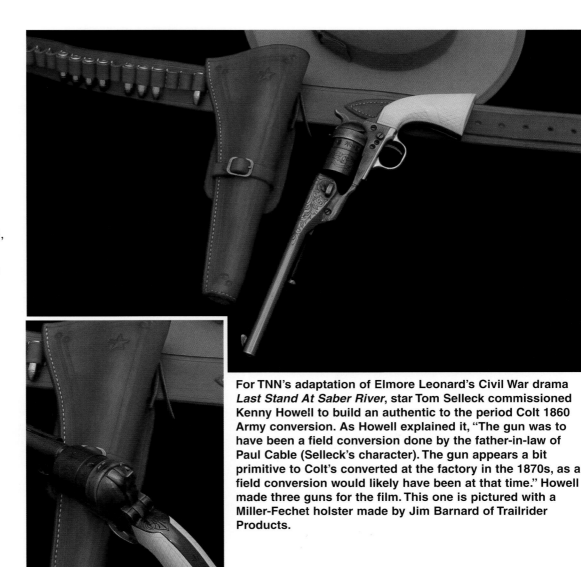

For TNN's adaptation of Elmore Leonard's Civil War drama *Last Stand At Saber River*, star Tom Selleck commissioned Kenny Howell to build an authentic to the period Colt 1860 Army conversion. As Howell explained it, "The gun was to have been a field conversion done by the father-in-law of Paul Cable (Selleck's character). The gun appears a bit primitive to Colt's converted at the factory in the 1870s, as a field conversion would likely have been at that time." Howell made three guns for the film. This one is pictured with a Miller-Fechet holster made by Jim Barnard of Trailrider Products.

In *Last Stand At Saber River*, Paul Cable looks at the 1860 Army cartridge conversion made for him by his father-in-law and says to his wife, while admiring the engraving and his name inscribed on the backstrap, "Your father's a real artist," to which his wife replies, "I did it, if you want to know."

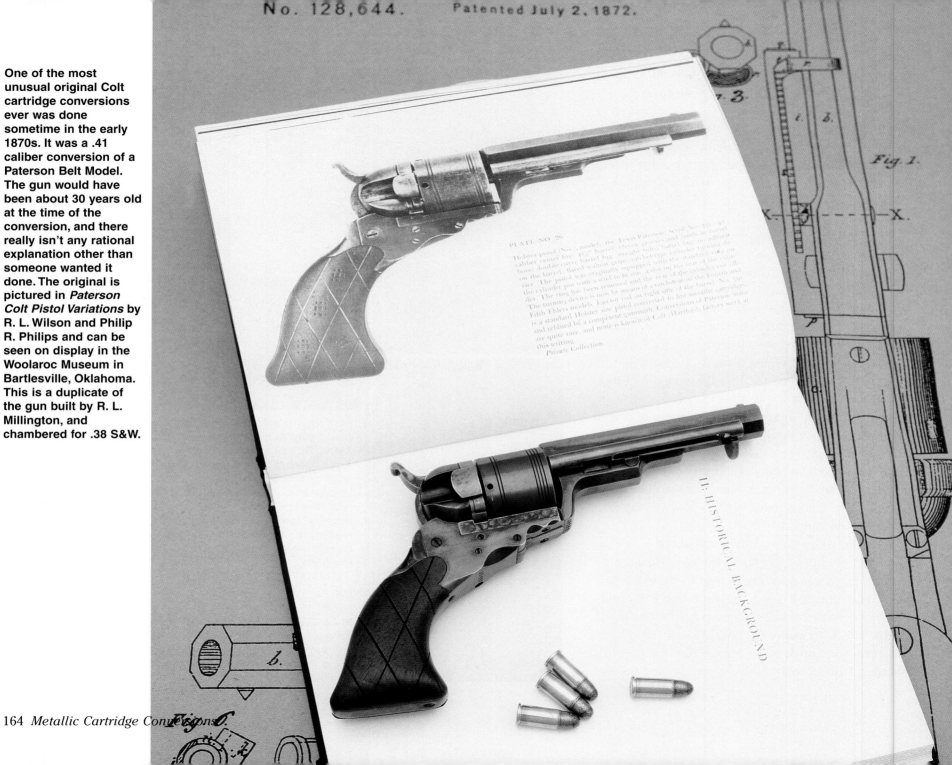

One of the most unusual original Colt cartridge conversions ever was done sometime in the early 1870s. It was a .41 caliber conversion of a Paterson Belt Model. The gun would have been about 30 years old at the time of the conversion, and there really isn't any rational explanation other than someone wanted it done. The original is pictured in *Paterson Colt Pistol Variations* by R. L. Wilson and Philip R. Philips and can be seen on display in the Woolaroc Museum in Bartlesville, Oklahoma. This is a duplicate of the gun built by R. L. Millington, and chambered for .38 S&W.

a threaded hole that allows a screw to secure it.

The next step is to take the frame and mill a channel in the right recoil plate for cartridge loading and extraction. A dovetail slot is then milled for the ejector housing. After that is done, Millington makes an ejector housing from 3/8th-inch square stock and fits it to the frame exactly as Remington factory gunsmiths did. Every gun is hand-built and each has a new, custom-fitted cylinder. After timing the gun and cutting the bolt slots, the last step is to reshape the face of the hammer into a firing pin.

Millington manufactures all of his own parts, does his own case hardening, and finishing, following the same steps and using the same techniques as Remington gunsmiths did at the Ilion, New York factory beginning in 1868.

"I like the Remingtons more than the Colts," admits Millington. "They're a sturdier, better-built gun, and easier to convert. The Colt is a weak type gun because of the open-top frame and the removable barrel. The Remington is just a better all around pistol."

Hardly anyone will argue the point. Remingtons are inherently better guns. The time that elapsed between the original Colt's design and the first Remington revolvers of 1858 allowed for improvements in the design of the frame, loading lever, and cylinder. Overall, a Remington is easier to load, and easier to convert to fire metallic cartridges.

Nearly all of Millington's conversions have antique finishes. When I went to pick up the Remington Army conversion pictured on the cover, there were two on Millington's workbench. I asked, "Which one is mine?" He said "The bottom one. The

The subtleties of authentic reproductions sometimes require aged finishes and attention to such details as serial numbering and inspector's marks. This First Model Richards 1860 Army with a 12-stop cylinder is a rare gun in its original form, and very few reproductions have been made. R. L. Millington built this superb example.

other gun is an original." They're that good. The only telltale evidence is the taller front sight and the incorrect grip screw escutcheon. Those on modern reproductions are round, whereas originals had two small projections to secure them in the wood.

Millington's Remington conversions are available in an original 1868-69 five-shot version, with or without ejector, and chambered for .45 Colt; the later six-shot .44 Colt version, or Navy models chambered

The accuracy of a reproduction can often be determined by comparing it to an original. That said, one of these is a real 12-stop 1860 Army Richards conversion; the other is a reproduction.

This is one of three 1871-72 Open Top revolvers Kenny Howell built for the TNN production of Louis L'Amour's *Crossfire Trail*. Howell copied a variety of original designs to arrive at the model used in the film. The revolver had a shortened barrel, dovetailed front sight, and early Navy-style gripstrap with ivory stocks. Jim Barnard of Trailrider Products reproduced a Mexican loop holster like the one worn by actor Tom Selleck in the film.

What may be the ultimate Colt reproduction was an 1871-72 Tiffany-style Open Top built by Dave Anderson in 1999. Only a few were produced. Mike Harvey of Cimarron F.A. Co. also had a similar example built by A. Uberti & Co. in 2001.

Dave Anderson's Tiffany Open Tops were originally valued at $5,000. One of the first examples is pictured with a spectacular double shoulder holster handcrafted by Bruce Daly of Buffalo Brothers in Mesa, Arizona.

for .38 Long Colt and .38 Special. Even though he manufactures new cylinders out of the highest-grade steel, for safety and to reduce wear on the guns, Millington recommends using only Black Hills ammunition or other reduced-pressure cowboy loads.

Colt cartridge conversions, such as the 1862 Pocket Police pictured in this chapter are another of Millington's specialties. Each is done in the authentic Richards-Mason conversion style. He has done 1851 Navy models, 1860 Army, Pocket Navy and Pocket Police models, Dragoons, Walkers, and several copies of the very rare Paterson conversion, as shown on page 60 of R.L. Wilson's book, *Paterson Colt Pistol Variations*.

"The Paterson is an unusual revolver to convert to metallic cartridge because of its design. It is far more difficult to build, and is best chambered for either .38 Colt or .38 Smith & Wesson, although the example pictured in Wilson's book was chambered for .41 Colt," said Millington.

As with all of Millington's cartridge conversions, his reproduction Paterson is true to the original, with the exception of caliber.

Millington's company, ArmSport LLC in Eastlake, Colorado, will custom convert any Colt or Remington model, (including original guns and Second Generation Colt Blackpowder models) and offers a number of custom finishes, antiquing, and hand engraving in the Nimschke style.

In the 21st century, R. L. Millington and Kenny Howell are about as close to finding a 19th century frontier gunsmith as you can get.

Cowboy Action Shooting

Today, Colt and Remington cartridge conversions are as popular among collectors, shooters and re-enactors as they were among frontiersmen in the 1870s. Reproductions of the Colt 1860 Army and 1858 Remington cartridge conversions have found a home in Cowboy Action Shooting. These weapons, like

Once again R. L. Millington's penchant for authenticity is exhibited in this 1858 Remington Army cartridge conversion shown with an original gun.

Dave Anderson converted a Rogers and Spencer to fire metallic cartridges for use in the movie *The Quick And The Dead*. The grips were decorated with tacks in an Indian motif. Actor Woody Strode carried it in the film.

R. L. Millington has built his business primarily on conversions of Remington Army and Navy models, which are not available from production manufacturers like A. Uberti & Co. Millington has been producing Remington cartridge conversions since 1995. Pictured are an 1858 New Model Army chambered for .45 Colt, and a Remington Navy chambered for .38 Colt.

Another of R.L. Millington's superb Remington conversions is this engraved example produced in 2002 for the Colorado Gun Collector's Association. Millington converted the Remington Army model to .44 Colt and engraved the gun in period motif. It is pictured with Jim Barnard's popular Miller-Fechet pattern holster.

pages torn from the history and lore of the Old West, ideally suit the authentic character of this rapidly growing shooting sport.

"It is the Single Action Shooting Society that has made the cartridge conversion revolver so popular," says Howell. "The only people that looked at cartridge conversions were those who were into the history of the Old West or gun collectors, and a lot of those same people went into Cowboy Action Shooting as the sport began to develop. Almost everyone used Colt SAA revolvers and Model 92s. Then all of a sudden they wanted Henrys and Model 66 Winchesters, cartridge conversions, break-open Smiths, and Merwin Hulbert revolvers. Cowboy Action Shooting has had more of an influence on

The Remington Navy model is one of R. L. Millington's favorite conversions and he has accurately duplicated the original design is every detail, particularly the loading gate and ejector which were first offered by Remington as a standard feature on this model. Note the loading gate latch and channeling of the recoil shield.

rekindling interest in historic guns than anything else, even movies."

In addition to Single Action Shooting Society matches, firearms collectors, and weekend plinkers have also become captivated by these historic recreations of the earliest cartridge-firing American revolvers.

"Within SASS and Cowboy Action Shooting," says Howell; "cartridge conversions are most popular among people concerned more with authenticity than

Remington & Sons offered a variety of percussion models in the 1860s, all of which were later converted to fire metallic cartridges. R. L. Millington builds reproductions of the four primary models; Army, Navy, Carbine, and Pocket Pistol, the latter chambered for .32 caliber centerfire cartridges. The Army and Carbine can be chambered for five .45 Colt rounds or six .44 Colt rounds, the Navy for six .38 Colt cartridges.

the actual ability to shoot fast with them. It takes a special person to use a cartridge conversion in SASS. It takes a person who is really steeped in history and is intent on recreating a time period with the clothing and the guns, someone who is more of an historian than a competitive shooter."

In serious competition a Colt or Remington cartridge conversion can't outperform a Colt Single Action Army, and adds Howell, "A Colt SAA can't outshoot a new Ruger Vaquero that has been tuned for competition. You can't beat one. But if you want

to play that era from the post-Civil War period to the early 1880s, you need to carry a Colt or Remington conversion."

Howell explains that in the 1870s the majority of people venturing west had very little money and a used Colt or Remington converted to metallic cartridge cost a lot less than a new Peacemaker.

"A Colt SAA was about $18, while a cartridge conversion revolver could be purchased for somewhere between $6 and $12," said Howell. "Colt and Remington took cap-and-ball revolvers and

Two of R. L. Millington's finest pieces replicate an original pair of Nimschke-engraved Pocket Navy conversions. Although the originals were .38 rimfire, the reproductions are chambered for .38 Colt centerfire.

converted them for a very reasonable price, both for the military and the public, and as a result they became the most common guns on the frontier throughout the 1870s and early 1880s. The cartridge conversion revolver was an important part of the post-Civil War era and made a significant contribution to our American heritage. Reproducing those guns today, pays homage to that great era."

Production Reproductions

While craftsmen like Gren, Howell and Millington were building custom cartridge conversions; the demand for these guns far outstripped their ability to produce sufficient quantities. Handcrafted conversions were just that, handcrafted, and they required considerable time to build and were expensive, averaging more than $1,000.

Into this scenario arrived gunsmith Dave Anderson, a former machinist who segued got into gunsmithing as second career in the late 1970s. Another follower of John Gren, Anderson opened a shop in Lakewood, California and began building

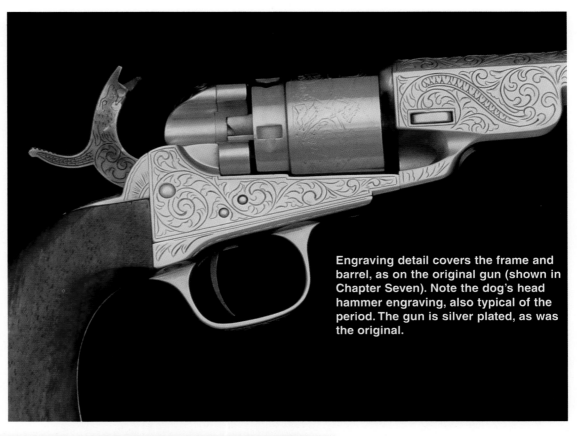

Engraving detail covers the frame and barrel, as on the original gun (shown in Chapter Seven). Note the dog's head hammer engraving, also typical of the period. The gun is silver plated, as was the original.

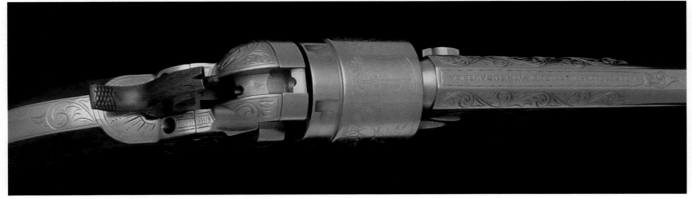

More engraving detail is shown in this view of the Pocket Navy conversion. By using a Second Generation Colt, greater authenticity can be achieved with correct barrel address and factory patent dates on the frame.

The Colt's workroom produced a number of experimental conversions in the late 1860s while awaiting the expiration of the Rollin White patent. This reproduction by R. L. Millington depicts one such experimental model. The one-off model was built to exhibit authentic antique finishing. It has an octagonal barrel half turned-round and a wedge firing pin held in place by two rivets. The gun is chambered for .44 centerfire.

A variety of Civil War era revolvers were converted from percussion to metallic cartridge, among which were a handful of Starr single-and double-action models. R. L. Millington has copied an original design c. 1872-1875 in which a breech ring containing a rebounding firing pin was fitted to the face of the recoil shield.

The chambers were bored through for .44 caliber centerfire cartridges, a new cylinder ratchet cut, and the hand altered. A cylinder arbor was also added to facilitate easier removal for loading and unloading. ➤

◄ The frame, however, still had to be opened and the cylinder removed each time the gun was loaded, thus the Starr conversion was not particularly successful. It does, however, make for an interesting contemporary conversion of the Italian-made single-action models manufactured by Pietta.

custom conversions. "I always liked Western guns the best," said Anderson, "and when the Single Action Shooting Society was formed I got in on the ground floor."

He recognized a need for greater production than independent gunsmiths could meet, and decided to attempt mass production by designing the conversion components and having them produced in Italy, where reproduction Colt and Remington percussion revolvers were being built.

Initially, he contracted with Armi San Marco to build the components—cylinders, barrels, and ejector housings—needed to quickly convert a percussion revolver. Anderson designed his own version of the Richards conversion ring with a floating firing pin, but without the lip extending over the cylinder, as on the original Richards breechring design.

Kenny Howell and the R&D Gunshop will be introducing a Remington Army conversion chambered for six .44 Colt cartridges. This prototype exhibits the fine attention to detail for which Howell has come to be known. The conversions should become available through Taylor's & Co. in 2003. Note that once again the firing pin has been fashioned from the percussion hammer. Howell also uses a breechplate slightly thicker than original.

Anderson produced both the First Model Richards and Mason-style ejectors, providing two distinct types of conversions. Unfortunately both utilized the later Richards-Mason style breechring

Handcrafted Colt's cartridge conversions can be very expensive, most more than $1,000. Lower-priced reproductions have been tried in the past but have not been successful, until now. A. Uberti & Co. (a division of Beretta) has begun manufacturing Richards-Mason conversions of the 1851 Navy, 1860 Army, and the 1871-72 Open Top. The Open Top model (bottom) is sold exclusively through Cimarron F.A. Co. in Fredericksburg, Texas. These reasonably priced reproductions retail for $469. The engraved Open Top shown retails for around $1,600.

fitted with a Richards rebounding firing pin, a historically incorrect but nonetheless intriguing idea.

Anderson produced very sturdy, well-made guns, in a wide variety of models, including a few Colt's never offered, like the author's one-of-a-kind nickel-plated 1861 Navy with a First Model Richards ejector. He also offered different barrel lengths, custom engraving and a handful of custom-built models including a spectacular 1872 Tiffany-style Open Top, and a Rogers and Spencer cartridge conversion, one of which was featured in the Gene Hackman, Sharon Stone western, *The Quick and the Dead*.

When Armi San Marco was purchased by American Western Arms in 2000, Anderson lost his parts supplier, although by the late 1990s Armi San Marco had also gone into the cartridge conversion business, selling guns similar to Anderson's through a variety of importers including Navy Arms, Traditions, and Cimarron F.A. Co. Sadly, the Italian-built copies lacked Dave Anderson's penchant for quality, fit and finish.

American Western Arms ended production shortly after acquiring the Italian manufacturing facilities and the supply of cartridge conversions that had suddenly appeared on the American market disappeared almost as quickly. Unfortunately, Dave Anderson's American Frontier Firearms was gone, too. It was back to the waiting lists for cartridge conversion enthusiasts who wanted to purchase a handcrafted revolver built by Howell or Millington. Gren had also ceased production by this time.

Italy's oldest and most respected manufacturer of reproduction black powder revolvers, Aldo Uberti & Co. was already producing a highly authentic

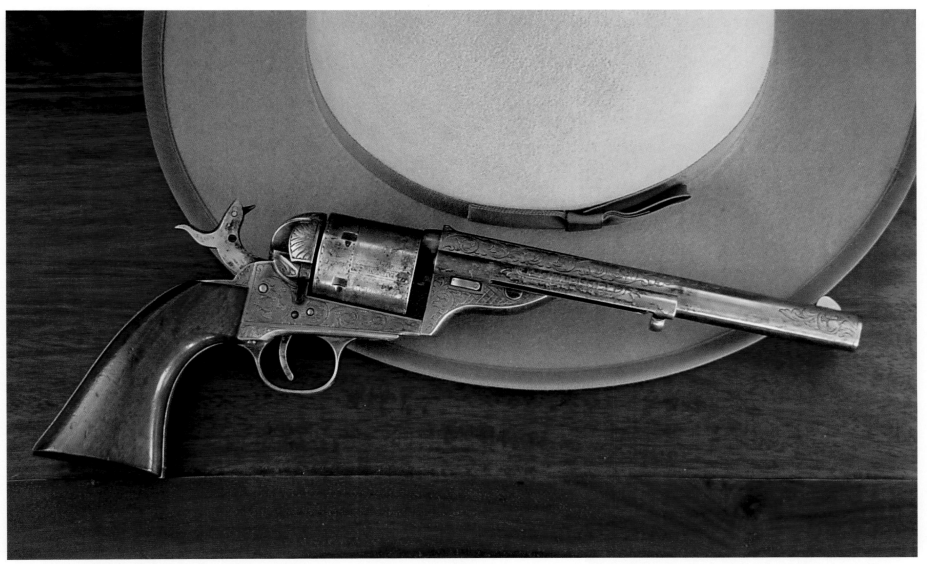

An interesting option offered for the Cimarron 1871-72 Open Top is an antique gray finish with "C" style engraving. Each gun is made to order and retails for $1,609. The antique finish adds an even more authentic look to the gun, which duplicates the original Colt design as closely as possible. One unique feature to the Cimarron models is an integral hammer lock activated by turning the screw (just ahead of the thumbpiece), releasing a safety bar that prevents the hammer from falling far enough forward for the firing pin to strike the cartridge.

About as fancy as a gun can get, Cimarron offers the Richards-Mason style 1860 Army with full engraving, nickel finish and white Micarta stocks. This deluxe special order model retails for $2,094. Above, a custom-built Open Top Tiffany produced by the artisans at Uberti and valued at more than $5,000.

Right side views of engraved
Cimarron Army and Open Top
revolvers exhibit the exceptional
workmanship of Italian engravers.

The last word in original Colt percussion and conversion models were those examples engraved by Gustave Young and Louis D. Nimschke and adorned with engraved cast grips. The design was originated by Tiffany but copied by others for sale though Schuyler, Hartley and Graham in New York City. The original design has been faithfully reproduced in this Uberti 1871-72 Open Top.

Solid-lug Army reproductions from Cimarron can be ordered with full engraving and nickel finish to rival the originals of the 1870s.

reproduction of the 1871-72 Open Top exclusively for Mike Harvey of Cimarron F.A. Co. in Fredericksburg, Texas. Harvey had gone to great lengths to ensure the accurate design of the Colt, with the necessary exception of having the guns chambered for centerfire cartridges. In 2002, the Open Tops were joined by a Richards-Mason-style conversion that is somewhat less than accurate but well made and reasonably priced, once again offering consumers a choice between a production gun and a handcrafted conversion.

Cimarron F.A. Co. has become the largest distributor of Uberti's Colt conversions, including a new reproduction of the Thuer 1860 Army model, introduced by Cimarron at the 2002 SHOT Show in Las Vegas.

Once again there is no shortage of cartridge conversion Colts for collectors, enthusiasts, and cowboy action shooters. It's the old theory supply and demand. And when it comes to the guns that won the West, there is definitely a demand.

Why Remingtons Make The Best Cartridge Conversions

The folks in Ilion, New York, knew what they were doing when they designed the Remington 1858 New Model Army revolver. It was stronger and better built than the Colt open-top design that had been around since the 1830s. The fixed barrel was an improvement, the topstrap made it more durable, and the cylinder could be changed out in a matter of seconds without taking the gun apart. That in and of itself made the Remington .44 a better sidearm during the Civil War.

The latest cartridge model from Uberti and Cimarron F.A. Co. is a reproduction of the Thuer 1860 Army. One of the true oddities in Colt's history, the Thuer used metallic cartridges pressed into the front of the cylinder with the loading lever (as a means of getting around the S&W Rollin White patent). After firing, an ejector lever (at the top of breech ring) was moved and the hammer cocked and dropped to eject each casing out of the cylinder.

Here are two different approaches to the same end. Walt Kirst manufactures a drop-in cartridge conversion cylinder for the 1858 Remington Army that is chambered for five .45 Colt cartridges. Kenny Howell has devised a means of getting six .45 rounds into a cylinder. Kirst uses a single rebounding firing pin in the cylinder cap. Howell has decided to use six separate pins. The Kirst cylinder rotates but the cap is locked in place to the frame, whereas, the entire cylinder and cap rotate together in the Howell design. They both perform well, making the distinction a matter of choice.

When it came to making the first cartridge conversion, Remington also had a better solution—a replaceable two-piece bored-through cylinder with a removable backplate. These were offered for the smaller-caliber Pocket, Police and Rider revolvers, which could be easily converted from cap-and-ball to rimfire metallic cartridge by changing the cylinder. A number of British patents for similar designs also appeared in the 1860s, principally those of J. Adams in 1861 and W. Tranter in 1865. Eli Whitney Jr. also patented a two-piece cylinder design in 1866, but Remington went to market with a two-piece cylinder of their own design in the early 1870s, allowing their percussion models to be loaded either way.

Kenny Howell and the R&D Gunshop build a somewhat unusual Remington conversion based on the early rimfire designs, which provides for a two-piece cylinder with an indexed backplate, containing six floating firing pins for centerfire cartridges. "We basically took the Remington design for the two-piece cylinder chambered for rimfire cartridges and turned it into a centerfire by using six firing pins," Howell said.

Howell's conversion design allows any Remington cap-and-ball pistol to be switched to .45 Colt in a matter of seconds. The drawback is that you must remove the cylinder to load and unload the gun, but compared to ejecting and loading six rounds in a Colt's revolver, reloading a two-piece cylinder takes a fraction of the time. How long? We timed it. To drop the loading lever, pull the cylinder pin, drop the cylinder, remove the backplate, dump the empty casings, drop in five new rounds (always leaving the sixth chamber empty as a safety measure), replace the backplate, put the cylinder back in, slide the pin home and slap the loading lever back in place takes an average of 20 seconds. To unload and reload a Colt conversion takes a total of 34 seconds.

The R&D conversion is available only for steel-frame Remington revolvers and is also offered for the Ruger Old Army. All conversion cylinders should only be fired with cowboy loads. The R&D cylinders are sold exclusively through Taylor's & Co. in Winchester, Va.

Taking a slightly different approach to the same idea is designer Walt Kirst of Kirst Company in Minneapolis, Minn., who has developed his own variation of the Adams and Tranter two-piece cylinder to fire five .45 Colt rounds. The Kirst Remington conversion is even faster to change

because of its unique breech ring design, which is flat on the bottom, immediately locking the cylinder into the frame. And since the Kirst breech ring has a single firing pin, it does not have to index with the cylinder. You simply push them together and drop the cylinder into the frame. On the average, a reload takes 16 seconds. With two cylinders, you can cut that to seven seconds.

Walt Kirst has developed a do-it-yourself conversion kit, which includes a new cylinder (chambered for either .45 Colt, .44 Colt, or .45 ACP), a channeled breechring, and a new cylinder arbor with an attached ejector. The kit also comes with precise instructions for channeling the recoil shield on a reproduction 1858 Remington Army. Following Kirst's directions and using only a rattail file and a Dremel tool, a breech-loading conversion can be built in one day.

Why five rounds instead of six? "The answer lies in the original Remington New Model Army conversions," says Kirst, "Insufficient space between the chambers for six .45 caliber rounds."

R&D's Ken Howell tackles the problem by boring the chambers at a very slight angle, thus increasing the clearance between the cartridge rims and allowing six rounds to be loaded. Bored from the rear to the front, the chamber (if viewed as a cutaway) has the cartridge slanting downward so that the bullet strikes the forcing cone (back of the barrel) at a slight angle. Howell explains that this has virtually no effect on the gun or bullet. For Cowboy Action shooting one needs to have an open chamber, so the sixth (empty) chamber, indicated by a silver firing pin, brings the R&D cylinder up to SASS standards.

Both the R&D and Kirst conversion cylinders functioned flawlessly in our test gun and delivered acceptable accuracy at 25 feet, grouping 10 shots all within the 8, 9, and 10 rings. R&D cylinders, available in .45 Colt (for 1858 Remington New Model Army revolvers and for the Ruger Old Army) and .38 Long Colt (for Remington Navy), are sold by Taylor's & Co., in Winchester, Va., and retail for $235. Kirst Konverters are available in .45 Colt from River Junction Trade Co., in McGregor, Iowa, and retail for $239.95.

Walt Kirst has taken things one step further with an idea that harkens back to the *The Legal Defender* of the 1960s. He now offers his conversion cylinder with a channeled breech ring and instructions for channeling the recoil shield, thereby creating a Remington conversion that can be loaded and unloaded at the breech. The directions are easy to follow and the work requires only simple tools, and one afternoon. The result is a Remington that, like the original models from the early 1870s, can fire metallic cartridges or be switched back to percussion simply by replacing the original cylinder.

In the end, it seems that nothing is really new, and that history does in fact repeat itself. For collectors of original cartridge conversions, for re-enactors and members of the Single Action Shooting Society, that's probably as it should be.

Kirst also offers a .38 caliber drop-in conversion cylinder for the Colt 1851 Navy. It is available as a drop-in only or with a channeled conversion ring for frame modification similar to the Remington.

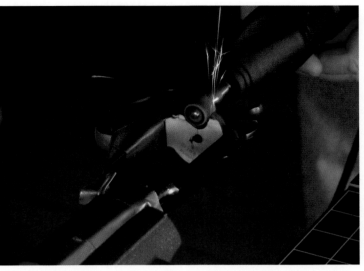

The first cut is the hardest. The file is used to open a channel in the recoil shield, which will be expanded with the Dremel tool and finally polished. The template, attached to the inside of the recoil shield shows the necessary depth of the channel.

The Dremel tool is used to widen and deepen the channel into the recoil shield until it reaches the template. This must be done in stages of about one minute at a time, allowing the metal to cool and to check the depth.

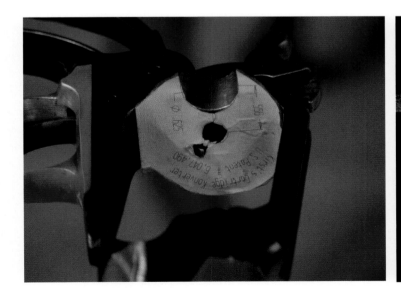

Once the channel has been cut, it needs to be polished with steel wool ending with #0000. After that the area can be cold blued, or as in this case, the entire gun can be polished or given an antique finish.

Here is another early conversion by John Gren on a Second Genration Colt Third Model Dragoon. Once again Gren used the First Model Richards-style hammer and a conversion ring combining elements of both the Richards Type I and Type II design. (Dennis Russell Collection)

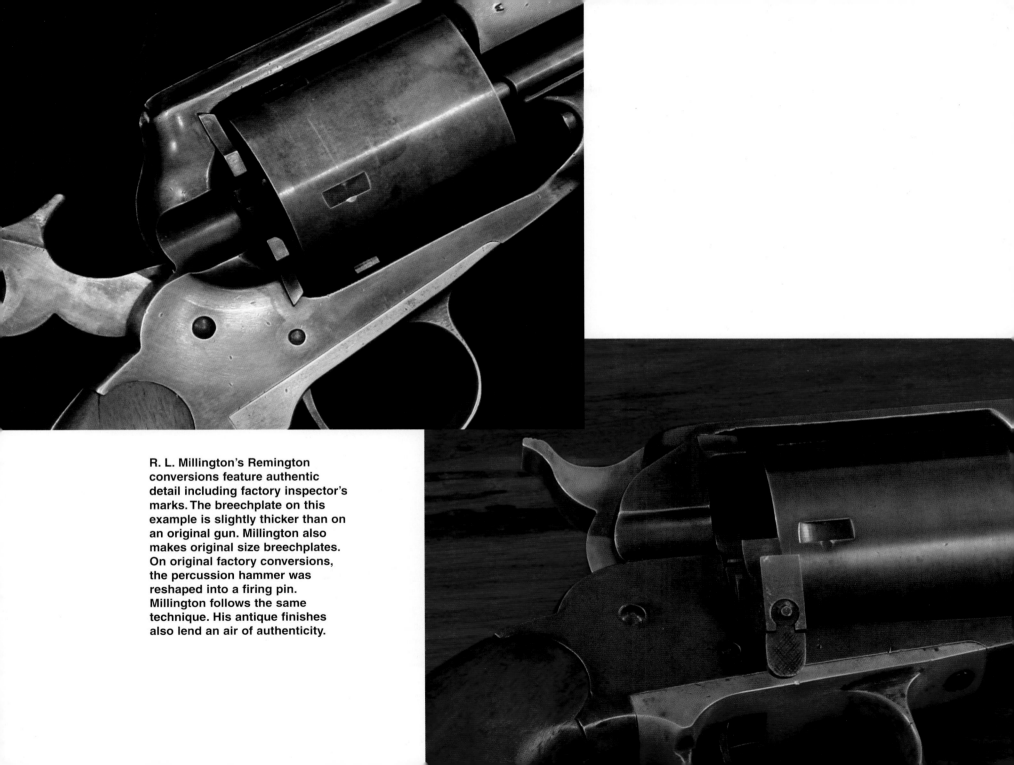

R. L. Millington's Remington conversions feature authentic detail including factory inspector's marks. The breechplate on this example is slightly thicker than on an original gun. Millington also makes original size breechplates. On original factory conversions, the percussion hammer was reshaped into a firing pin. Millington follows the same technique. His antique finishes also lend an air of authenticity.

Wild Bill Hickok carried a pair of Colt 1851 Navy revolvers butt forward in a double holster rig. His legendary double reverse draw cost many a gunslinger their life. Jim Barnard of Trailrider Products recreated the Hickock holsters and belt for reproductions chapter in this book.

Two guns in one. Walt Kirst developed a drop-in cartridge cylinder for the Colt 1851 Navy, thus allowing one gun to serve as either a percussion or cartridge revolver depending upon the cylinder. R. L. Millington takes the Kirst guns and refinishes them with a channeled breech ring and recoil shield, new case hardened frame and blued finish. The custom Kirst-Millington 1851 Navy models are the best of both worlds.

In Sam Peckinpah's 1965 film *Major Dundee*, starring Charlton Heston, Major Amos Dundee carried a First Model Richards 1860 Army conversion.

CHAPTER 11

Movies, Television, and Cowboy Action Shooting

Bringing Authenticity to the Screen and Shooting Hobby

The cowboy life is a theme as old as the cinema itself. The cowboy heroes of the silent screen always wore white hats. Later on, William Boyd, a.k.a. Hopalong Cassidy, changed that image by wearing all black and a black hat. But the image of the good guy in the white hat and the villains, or heroes with a taint of evil, in black still persists.

Back in the heyday of the Western serial or silver-screen epic, not a great deal of attention was given to authentic wardrobe, guns or holsters. Almost everyone, from heroes to desperados carried a Colt Single Action Army. The good guys occasionally got a silver-plated Peacemaker. But it was rare that you ever saw anything but an 1873 Colt SAA in any films.

Cecil B. DeMille was perhaps one of the first great film directors to use period correct guns in a Western. It was 1942 and the film was *Reap The Wild Wind* starring Raymond Massey and Robert Preston. In the film Massey carried a real Colt Paterson revolver.

The next memorable image of a period correct gun other than a SAA was in Sam Peckinpah's 1965 epic *Major Dundee* starring Charlton Heston as Major Amos Dundee. In the film Heston carried a First Model Richards 1860 Army conversion. Heston still owns the gun.

Back in the 1960s there weren't any reproduction cartridge conversions, so real 1870s guns were restored and tuned by the studio prop departments. Another original First Model Richards turned up on Bonanza during the early shows. Pernell Roberts, who played Adam Cartwright, carried it. Hoss and Ben got new Colt SAA revolvers and Little Joe was stuck with an 1851 Navy percussion revolver.

In this early promotional still a young Pernell Roberts (second from left) is holding an original Richards 1860 Army cartridge conversion. Brother Hoss (Dan Blocker) and father Ben Cartwright (Loren Green) both carried Colt SAA revolvers, and Little Joe, played by a very young Michael Landon (far right) got to carry a hand-me-down 1851 Navy percussion revolver.

Clint Eastwood wielded a Remington Army cartridge conversion in the 1985 Warner Bros. film *Pale Rider*. In what has to be one of the most memorable shootouts in any Western, he calmly dropped the loading lever, pulled the cylinder pin forward and switched to a second loaded cylinder (seen in his left hand), in the middle of a gunfight.

In *Crossfire Trail* Tom Selleck played Rafe Covington, a man of his word, and the word was to look after the wife of a friend who died in his arms. In the opening scene of the film, Covington exacts revenge on the man who killed his friend, and takes his gun, the ivory gripped 1871-72 Open Top, featured throughout the rest of the film.

It was Clint Eastwood who really brought authenticity to the Western. Early in his film career doing Sergio Leone's famed spaghetti westerns, Eastwood got a feel for authentic guns in his Italian surroundings where most of the reproduction black powder Colts were being built. They were prominently featured in *The Good, The Bad and The Ugly*, and in later Eastwood films like *The Outlaw Josey Wales* in which Eastwood carried an armory of large- and small-caliber Colt Dragoons and Pocket Pistols. The tradition for authenticity was established.

A great gun could almost steal the scene and Eastwood knew it. This was ideally portrayed in the 1985 film *Pale Rider* where Eastwood's "Preacher" carried a Remington Army conversion with a set of extra cylinders on his belt. Just before the final confrontation in the movie he is shown sitting at a table loading the cylinders. In the climactic final shootout Eastwood calmly changes cylinders in the middle of a gunfight, literally mesmerizing his opponent. It is one of the most memorable scenes in Western filmmaking.

In today's movies authenticity is a still the first order of business for most directors and actors, at least those who are gun enthusiasts and research their characters. Tom Selleck is perhaps the dean of this genre, ensuring that everything—from clothing to guns—is correct for the period. Much of that responsibility falls on Kenny Howell.

With quality reproductions any gun can be built to exacting standards for a film. For *Last Stand at Saber River* Howell built the 1860 Army conversion that was prominently featured in the opening of the film. For *Crossfire Trail* it was an 1871-72 Open Top, again prominently featured in the beginning of the film, and throughout. It is the gun that Rafe Covington (Selleck) finally uses to shoot hired assassin Bo Dorn (played by Brad Johnson).

A Western gun is more than a movie prop, it has become an integral part of modern filmmaking, and the exemplary reproductions on today's market have contributed to a new and higher standard. This is something that gun collectors, Western history aficionados, film buffs, re-enactors, and members of the Single Action Shooting Society can truly appreciate. Even more so, is the fact that guns of similar design can be enjoyed today, both on and off the silver screen.

I once said in a book that we are all frustrated actors. Members of the Single Action Shooting Society occasionally get to live the part. This is as close as I'll ever come to being Val Kilmer in *Tombstone*!

Jim Barnard of Trailrider Products copied the holster worn by Tom Selleck in *Crossfire Trail* to match the 1871-72 Open Top built by Kenny Howell. Howell hand-built the gun to original designs. Three guns were made for the film.

Beautiful checkered ivory stocks were made for the 1860 Army Richards conversion used by Tom Selleck in *Last Stand At Saber River*. Kenny Howell built the gun from a Second Generation Colt. Once again three identical guns were made for the movie.

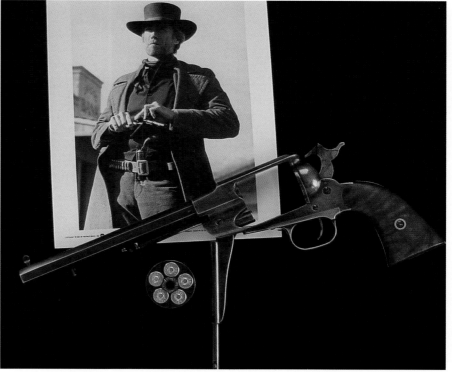

Clint Eastwood made it look easy to change a Remington cylinder in *Pale Rider*.

Appendix I

Trademark Index to Modern Gunsmiths, Manufacturers, and Suppliers

ARM SPORT LLC
Colt and Remington cartridge conversions
R. L. Millington/Gunmaker
P.O. Box 254
Eastlake, CO 80614
Phone No.: 303 451-7212
Web Site: www.armsportllc.com
Email: rlmillington@armsportllc.com

BLACK HILLS AMMUNITION
3050 Eglin St., P.O. Box 3090
Rapid City, SD 67709-3090
Phone No.: 605 348-5150
Fax No.: 605 348-9827
Email: bhammo@rapidnet.com
Web Site: www.black-hills.com

BUFFALO BROTHERS
Bruce Daly
Custom holsters and grips
8315 E. Quill St.
Mesa, AZ 85207
Phone No.: 480 986-7858
Web Site: www.buffalobrothers.net

CIMARRON, F.A. CO., INC.
105 Winding Oak, P.O. Box 906
Fredericksburg, TX 78624-0906
Phone No.: 830-997-9090
Fax No.: 830-997-0802
Web Site: www.cimarron-firearms.com
Email: cimarron@fbg.net

COWS (Classic Old West Styles)
Manufacturer of Authentic Western Clothing and
Accessories.
1060 Doniphan Park Circle, Suite C
El Paso, TX 79922
Phone No.: 800-595-2697
Fax No.: 915 587-0616
Web site: www.cows.com

P.W. & M.E. CRAVENER
Handcrafted reproductions of flintlock
pistols and longrifles
1252 Mission Rd.
Latrobe, PA 15650
Phone No.: 724-539-7667

DAY, LEONARD
Handcrafted reproductions of flintlock and swivel
barrel pistols and longrifles
3 Kings Highway,
West Hampton, MA 01027
Phone No.: 413-527-9627.

EL PASO SADDLERY CO.
Holster Makers since 1889
P.O. Box 27194
El Paso, TX 79926
Phone No.: 915 544-2233
Fax No.: 915 544-2535
Web site: www.epsaddlery.com

KIRST KONVERSION CYLINDER
Drop-in cartridge conversion
for 1858 Remington Army
River Junction Trade Co.
312 Main Street
McGreggor, IA 52257
Phone No.: 319-873-2387

KIRKPATRICK LEATHER
Holster Makers
P.O. Box 677
Laredo, TX 78042-0677
Phone No.: 956-723-6893
Fax No.: 956-725-0672

PEDERSOLI, DAVIDE & C.
Imported by Flintlocks, Etc.
160 Rossiter Rd.
Richmond, MA 01254
Phone No.: 413-698-3822
Fax No.: 413-698-3866
Email: flintetc@berkshire.rr.com
Pedersoli, Davide & C.
Via Artigiani 57
I-25063 Gardone V.T. (BS), ITALY
Fax No.: 011-39-30-8911019
Web site: www.davide-pedersoli.com

R&D GUNS
Ken Howell
Colt and Remington cartridge conversions, (For R&D
Remington "drop-in" conversion cylinders see
Taylor's & Co.)
5728 E. County Road X.
Beloit, WI 53511-9546
Phone No.: 608-676-5628
Fax No.: 608-676-2269

SHROYER ACCOUTREMENTS
Steve and Susan Shroyer
Hand-carved 18th & 19th century Powder Horns,
Hand-made hunting and game bags,
axes, and knives
157 Lake Drive
Bedford, PA 15522
Phone No.: 814-623-2535

TAYLOR'S & CO., INC.
304 Lenoir Dr.
Winchester, VA 22603
Phone No.: 540-722-2017
Fax No.: 540-722-2018
Email: info@taylorsfirearms.com
Web Site: www.taylorsfirearms.com

TRAILRIDER PRODUCTS
Jim Barnard
Original-style Western holsters
P.O. Box 2284
Littleton, CO 80161
Phone No.: 303-791-6068
Fax No.: 303-683-5357
Email: trailrider@ecentral.com
Web Site: www.gunfighter.com/trailrider

UBERTI, ALDO & C., S.r.l.
Importer - Uberti USA, Inc.
P.O. Box 509
362 Limerock Road
Lakeville, CT 06039
Phone No.: 860-435-8068
Fax No.: 860-435-8146
Email: mail@uberti.com
Web Site: www.uberti.com
Factory - Aldo Uberti & C., S.r.l.
Via G. Carducci, 41
I-25068 Ponte Zanano (BS) ITALY
Email: uberti@lumetel.it

Index

Bibliography

The Book of Colt Firearms by R. L. Wilson, 1993 Blue Book Publications, Minneapolis, MN.

Steel Canvas-The Art of American Arms by R. L. Wilson, 1995 Random House, New York, NY.

A Study of Colt Conversions and Other Percussion Revolvers by R. Bruce McDowell, 1997 Krause Publications, Iola, WI.

Variations of Colt's New Model Police and Pocket Breech Loaders by John D. Breslin, William Q. Pirie, and David E. Price, 2002 Andrew Mobray Publishers.

Standard Catalog of Smith & Wesson by Jim Supica and Richard Nahas, 1996 Krause Publications, Iola, WI.

Flayderman's Guide to Antique American Firearms…and their values 7th Edition by Norm Flayderman, 1998 Krause Publications, Iola, WI.

Packing Iron by Richard C. Rattenbury, 1993 Zion International Publishing Company, Millwood, NY.

Colt Blackpowder Reproductions & Replicas, A Collector's & Shooter's Guide by Dennis Adler, 1998 Blue Book Publications, Inc. Minneapolis, MN.

Blue Book of Modern Black Powder Values 2nd Edition by Dennis Adler, 2002 Blue Book Publications, Inc. Minneapolis, MN.

Handguns of the World by Edward C. Ezell, 1981 Barnes & Noble Books, Stackpole Books.